AN ANTHOLOGY OF ENGLISH PROSE

1400–1900

AN ANTHOLOGY OF
ENGLISH PROSE
1400-1900

EDITED BY

EIRIAN JAMES

CAMBRIDGE
AT THE UNIVERSITY PRESS
1956

PUBLISHED BY

THE SYNDICS OF THE CAMBRIDGE UNIVERSITY PRESS

London Office: Bentley House, N.W. 1
American Branch: New York

Printed in the Netherlands
by Joh. Enschedé en Zonen ⁄ Haarlem

CONTENTS

CONTENTS

CONTENTS

PUBLISHER'S NOTE

Tape recordings and 78 r. p. m. records of each of the extracts in this anthology are available. Information about prices and supply can be had from the Director, Recorded Sound Department, The British Council, 65 Davies Street, London, W. 1.

Long-playing records are issued by Caedmon Publishers, 277 Fifth Avenue, New York 16, N. Y.

PREFACE

THE aim of this anthology is to introduce English prose literature to both foreign and English readers through the medium of the ear in consort with the printed text. It is planned for recording on thirty records and this has of necessity imposed limits on the length of the passages. Poems have their own unity; the form of an extract from prose is to some extent artificially imposed. Nevertheless an idea, an episode, a description, can have its curve of tension, its completed form, and an attempt has been made to achieve this.

Brevity imposes limitations. By-paths, however inviting, have had to be resisted, and dramatic prose and works of a purely scientific or philosophic nature have been alto- gether omitted. The passages have been arranged in rough chronological order, occasionally violated for purposes of comparison, but the collection of records clearly has a fluidity not revealed by the printed text. The barriers of the centuries can more easily be broken down for contrast and comparison.

Although the historical approach has its pitfalls, the notes are intended to place the writing within the context of its period and the life of the writer. While making decisions on individual authors, the general scheme has been borne in mind, and as many genres and types of writing as possible have been included. If the anthology represents the cadences of English prose in all its variety of style and rhythm, if it titillates the reader to explore the books from which the passages are taken, it will have achieved its purpose.

The recordings were made at Cambridge by members of the University under the direction of George Rylands, Fellow of King's College, to whom I am greatly indebted for his enthusiasm, advice and co-operation.

EIRIAN JAMES

LONDON, *3 February 1956*.

TEXTS

To help the foreign reader, the spelling and punctuation of the passages have been modernised, though the archaic forms of some words have been retained. Cuts are indicated.

A list of the most accessible editions is given on p. 203. In cases where the text has been taken from a different edition, this is indicated.

For permission to use copyright material we are indebted to the following: the Clarendon Press for an extract from the Earl of Clarendon's *History of the Great Rebellion;* Messrs Secker and Warburg for an extract from O. Lawson Dick's edition of John Aubrey's *Brief Lives;* Messrs P. J. and A. E. Dobell for an extract from Thomas Traherne's *Centuries of Meditations;* Messrs Constable and Co. Ltd. for an extract from George Meredith's *The Egoist;* the Trustees of the Hardy Estate and Messrs Macmillan and Co. for an extract from Thomas Hardy's *Tess of the d'Urbervilles.*

E. J.

SIR THOMAS MALORY

? 1406–71

Le Morte d'Arthur

(Probably finished in 1469–70; Caxton edition published in 1485)

... [THEN Sir Launcelot] departed and rode westerly, and there he sought a seven or eight days; and at the last he came to a nunnery, and then was Queen Guenever ware of Sir Launcelot as he walked in the cloister. And when she saw him there she swooned thrice, that all the ladies and gentlewomen had work enough to hold the queen up. So when she might speak, she called ladies and gentlewomen to her, and said: Ye marvel, fair ladies, why I make this fare. Truly, she said, it is for the sight of yonder knight that yonder standeth; wherefore I pray you all call him to me. When Sir Launcelot was brought to her, then she said to all the ladies: Through this man and me hath all this war been wrought, and the death of the most noblest knights of the world; for through our love that we have loved together is my most noble lord slain. Therefore, Sir Launcelot, wit thou well I am set in such a plight to get my soul-heal; and yet I trust through God's grace that after my death to have a sight of the blessed face of Christ, and at domesday to sit on his right side, for as sinful as ever I was are saints in heaven. Therefore, Sir Launcelot, I require thee and beseech thee heartily, for all the love that ever was betwixt us, that thou never see me more in the visage; and I command thee, on God's behalf, that thou forsake my company, and to thy kingdom thou turn again, and keep well thy realm from war and wrack; for as well as I have loved thee, mine heart will not serve me to see thee, for through thee and me is the flower of kings and knights destroyed; therefore, Sir Launcelot, go to thy realm, and there take thee a wife, and live with her with joy and bliss: and I pray thee heartily, pray for me to our Lord that I may amend my misliving. Now, sweet madam, said Sir Launcelot, would ye that I should now return again unto my country, and there to wed a lady? Nay, madam, wit you well that shall I never do, for I shall never be so false to you of that I have promised; but the same destiny that ye have taken you to, I will take me unto, for to please Jesu, and ever for you I cast me specially to pray. If thou wilt do so, said the queen, hold thy promise, but I may never believe but that thou wilt turn to the world again. Well, madam, said he, ye say as pleaseth you, yet wist you me never false of my promise, and God defend but I should forsake the world as ye have done. For in the quest of the Sangreal I had forsaken the vanities of the world had not your lord been. And if I had done so at that time, with my heart, will, and thought, I had passed all the knights that were in the Sangreal except Sir Galahad, my son. And therefore, lady, sithen ye have taken you to perfection, I must needs take me to perfection, of right. For I take record of God, in you I have had mine earthly joy; and if I had found you now so disposed, I had cast to have had you into mine own realm. [Chapter x] But sithen

I find you thus disposed, I ensure you faithfully, I will ever take me to penance, and pray while my life lasteth, if I may find any hermit, either gray or white, that will receive me. Wherefore, madam, I pray you kiss me and never no more. Nay, said the queen, that shall I never do, but abstain you from such works: and they departed. But there was never so hard an hearted man but he would have wept to see the dolour that they made; for there was lamentation as they had been stung with spears; and many times they swooned, and the ladies bare the queen to her chamber. And Sir Launcelot awoke, and went and took his horse, and rode all that day and all night in a forest, weeping.

JOHN BOURCHIER, LORD BERNERS
1467–1533
Sir John Froissart: Of the Chronicles of England, France, Spain, Portugal, Scotland, Brittany, Flanders, and other places adjoining

Translated out of French into our maternal English tongue, by John Bourchier Knight, Lord Berners: at the commandment of our most high redoubted sovereign Lord King Henry VIII, King of England and of France, and high Defender of the Christian Faith etc.

(First edition 1523–5)

HOW KING RICHARD YIELDED HIMSELF TO THE EARL OF DERBY TO GO TO LONDON. VOL. II, PART IV, CAP. CCXLII

IN the mean season while the king sat at dinner, who did eat but little, his heart was so full that he had no lust to eat.

All the country about the castle was full of men of war. They within the castle might see them out at the windows, and the king when he rose from the table might see them himself. Then he demanded of his cousin what men they were that appeared so many in the fields. The earl answered and said, the most part of them be Londoners. What would they have quoth the king? They will have you quoth the earl, and bring you to London and put you in the Tower, there is none other remedy, ye can scape none otherwise. No quoth the king and he was sore afraid of those words, for he knew well that the Londoners loved him not, and said. Cousin, can you not provide for my surety: I will not gladly put me into their hands. For I know well that they hate me and have done long, though I be their king. Then the earl said, Sir, I see none other remedy, but to yield yourself as my prisoner: and when they know that ye be my prisoner they will do you no hurt, but ye must so ordain you and your company to ride to London with me, and to be as my prisoner in the Tower of London. The king who saw himself in a hard case, all his spirits were sore abashed, as that he doubted greatly that the Londoners would slay him. Then he yielded himself prisoner to the earl of Derby and bound himself, and promised to do all that he would have him to do. In likewise all other knights, squires, and officers yielded to the earl, to eschew the danger and peril that they were in, and the earl then received them as his prisoners, and ordained incontinent horses to be saddled and brought forth into the court and the gates opened; then many men of arms and archers entered. Then the earl of Derby caused a cry to be made,

on pain of death, no man to be so hardy to take away
anything within the castle, nor to lay any hands upon any
person, for all were under the earl's safeguard and protection: which cry was kept; no man durst break it. The
earl had the king down into the court talking together,
and caused all the king's whole household and estate to
go forward, as of custom they had done before, without
changing or minishing of any thing. While everything was
a-preparing, the king and the earl communed together in
the court, and were well regarded by the Londoners. And
as it was informed me, King Richard had a greyhound
called Mathe, who always waited upon the king, and would
know no man else. For whensoever the king did ride, he
that kept the greyhound did let him loose, and he would
straight run to the king and fawn upon him, and leap
with his forefeet upon the king's shoulders. And as the
king and the earl of Derby talked together in the court,
the greyhound who was wont to leap upon the king, left
the king and came to the earl of Derby, duke of Lancaster,
and made to him the same friendly countenance and cheer,
as he was wont to do to the king. The duke who knew not
the greyhound, demanded of the king what the greyhound
would do. Cousin, quoth the king, it is a great good token
to you, and an evil sign to me. Sir, how know you that
quoth the duke. I know it well quoth the king. The
greyhound maketh you cheer this day as King of England,
as ye shall be, and I shall be deposed: the greyhound hath
this knowledge naturally, therefore take him to you, he
will follow you and forsake me. The duke understood well
those words and cherished the greyhound, who would

never after follow King Richard, but followed the duke of Lancaster.

SIR THOMAS MORE
1478–1535

Utopia

(Originally published in Latin in 1516; and in the translation of Ralph Robynson in 1551)

The Second Book of the 'Communication of Raphael Hythlodaye', concerning the best state of a common wealth, containing the description of Utopia, with a large declaration of the politic government, and of all the good laws and orders of the same island.

V. OF THEIR LIVING AND MUTUAL CONVERSATION TOGETHER

... BUT now again to the conversation of the citizens among themselves. The eldest ... ruleth the family. The wives be ministers to their husbands, the children to their parents, and to be short, the younger to their elders. Every city is divided into four equal parts. In the middle of every quarter there is a market place of all manner of things. Thither the works of every family be brought in to certain houses. And every kind of thing is laid up several in barns or store houses. From hence the father of every family or every householder fetcheth whatsoever he and his have need of, and carrieth it away with him without money, without exchange, without any gage or pledge. For why should any thing be denied unto him seeing there is abundance of all things, and that it is not to be feared lest any man will ask more than he needeth. For why should it be thought that that man would ask more than enough, which is sure never to lack? Certainly in all kinds of living creatures, either fear of lack doth cause covetousness and ravin, or in man only pride; which counteth it a glorious thing to pass and excel others in the superfluous and vain ostentation of things. The which kind of vice among the Utopians can have no place . . .

Moreover every street hath certain great large halls . . . [where] dwell the Syphogrants. And to every one of the same halls be appointed thirty families, of either side fifteen. The stewards of every hall at a certain hour come in to the meat markets, where they receive meat according to the number of their halls. . . .

To these halls at the set hours of dinner and supper cometh all the whole Syphogranty or ward, warned by the noise of a brazen trumpet; except such as be sick in the hospitals or else in their own houses. Howbeit, no man is prohibited or forbid, after the halls be served, to fetch home meat out of the market to his own house. For they know that no man will do it without a cause reasonable. For though no man be prohibited to dine at home, yet no man doth it willingly, because it is counted a point of small honesty. And also it were a folly to take the pain to dress a bad dinner at home, when they may be welcome to good and fine fare so nigh hand at the hall. In this hall all vile service, all slavery and drudgery, with all laboursome toil and business, is done by bondmen. But the women of every family by course have the office and charge of cookery, for seething and dressing the meat and ordering all things thereto belonging. They sit at three tables or more according to the number of their company. The men sit upon the bench next the wall, and the women against them on the other side of the table: that, if any sudden evil should chance to them, as many times happeneth to women with child, they may rise without trouble or disturbance of anybody, and go thence into the nursery.

The nurses sit several alone with their young sucklings in a certain parlour appointed and deputed to the same purpose, never without fire and clean water, nor yet without cradles; that when they will they may lay down the young infants, and at their pleasure take them out of their swathing clothes, and hold them to the fire, and refresh them with play. Every mother is nurse to her own child, unless either death or sickness be the let. When that chanceth, the wives of the Syphogrants quickly provide a nurse. And that is not hard to be done. For they that can do it do proffer themselves to no service so gladly as to that. Because that there this kind of pity is much praised; and the child that is nourished ever after taketh his nurse for his own natural mother.

RICHARD HAKLUYT
? 1552–1616
Principal Navigations, Voyages and Discoveries of the English Nation
(First edition 1589; enlarged edition 1598–1600)

A report of the Voyage, and success thereof, attempted in the year of our Lord 1583, by Sir Humfrey Gilbert, Knight, with other gentlemen assisting him in that action, intended to discover and to plant Christian inhabitants in place convenient, upon those large and ample countries extended northward from the Cape of Florida, lying under very temperate climes, esteemed fertile and rich in minerals, yet not in the actual possession of any Christian prince. Written by Mr Edward Hayes, gentleman, and principal actor in the same voyage, who alone continued unto the end, and by God's special assistance, returned home with his retinue safe and entire.

... LEAVING the issue of this good hope unto God, who knoweth the truth only, and can at His good pleasure bring the same to light, I will hasten to the end of this tragedy, which must be knit up in the person of our General. And as it was God's ordinance upon him, even so the vehement persuasion and entreaty of his friends could nothing avail to divert him of a wilful resolution of going through in his frigate; which was overcharged upon the decks with fights, nettings, and small artillery, too cumbersome for so small a boat that was to pass through the ocean sea at that season of the year, when by course we might expect much storm of foul weather. Whereof indeed we had enough.

But when he was entreated by the captain, master, and other his well-willers of the *Hind* not to venture in the frigate, this was his answer: *I will not forsake my little company going homeward, with whom I have passed so many storms and perils.* And in very truth he was urged to be so over hard by hard reports given of him that he was afraid of the sea; albeit this was rather rashness than advised resolution, to prefer the wind of a vain report to the weight of his own life. Seeing he would not bend to reason, he had provision out of the *Hind,* such as was wanting aboard his frigate. And so we committed him to God's protection, and set him aboard his pinnace, we being more than 300 leagues onward of our way home.

By that time we had brought the Islands of Azores south of us; yet we then keeping much to the north, until we had got into the height and elevation of England, we met with very foul weather and terrible seas, breaking short and high, pyramid-wise. The reason whereof seemed to proceed either of hilly grounds high and low within the sea, as we see hills and vales upon the land, upon which the seas do mount and fall, or else the cause proceedeth of diversity of winds, shifting often in sundry points, all which having power to move the great ocean, which again is not presently settled, so many seas do encounter together, as there had been diversity of winds. Howsoever it cometh to pass, men which all their lifetime had occupied the sea never saw more outrageous seas. We had also upon our mainyard an apparition of a little fire by night, which seamen do call *Castor* and *Pollux*. But we had only one, which they take an evil sign of more tempest; the same is usual in storms.

Monday, the 9th of September, in the afternoon, the frigate was near cast away, oppressed by waves, yet at that time recovered; and giving forth signs of joy, the General sitting abaft with a book in his hand, cried out to us in the *Hind*, so oft as we did approach within hearing, *We are as near to heaven by sea as by land*. Reiterating the same speech, well beseeming a soldier resolute in Jesus Christ, as I can testify he was.

The same Monday night, about twelve of the clock, or not long after, the frigate being ahead of us in the *Golden Hind*, suddenly her lights were out, whereof as it were in a moment we had lost the sight, and withal our watch cried *the General was cast away*, which was too true. For in that moment the frigate was devoured and swallowed up of the sea. Yet still we looked out all that night, and ever after until we arrived upon the coast of England. . . .

SIR THOMAS NORTH
1535 ?–1601 ?

The Lives of the Noble Grecians and Romans, compared together by that Learned Philosopher and Historiographer Plutarch of Chaeronea

Translated out of Greek into French by James Amyot, Abbot of Bellozane, Bishop of Auxerre, one of the King's Privy Council, and Great Aumer of France, and out of French into English by Thomas North.

(First edition 1579)

THE LIFE OF MARCUS ANTONIUS

THE manner how he fell in love with her was this. Antonius, going to make war with the Parthians, sent to command Cleopatra to appear personally before him when he came into Cilicia, to answer unto such accusations as were laid against her, being this: that she had aided Cassius and Brutus in their war against him. The messenger sent unto Cleopatra to make this summons unto her was called Dellius: who when he had thoroughly considered her beauty, the excellent grace and sweetness of her tongue, he nothing mistrusted that Antonius would do any hurt to so noble a lady, but rather assured himself that within few days she should be in great favour with him. Thereupon he did her great honour, and persuaded her to come into Cilicia as honourably furnished as she could possible, and bade her not to be afraid at all of Antonius, for he was a more courteous lord than any she had ever seen. Cleopatra, on the other side, believing Dellius' words, and guessing by the former access and credit she had with Julius Caesar and Cneius Pompey (the son of Pompey the Great) only for her beauty, she began to have good hope that she might more easily win Antonius. For Caesar and Pompey knew her when she was but a young thing, and knew not then what the world meant: but now she went to Antonius at the age when a woman's beauty is at the prime, and she also of best judgment. So she furnished herself with a world of gifts, store of gold and silver, and of riches and other sumptuous ornaments, as is credible enough she might bring from so great a house, and from so wealthy and rich a realm as Egypt was. But yet she carried nothing with her wherein she trusted more than in herself, and in the charms and enchantment of her passing beauty and grace. Therefore when she was sent unto by divers letters, both from Antonius himself, and also from his friends, she made so light of it and mocked Antonius so much, that she disdained to set forward otherwise, but to take her barge in the river of Cydnus, the poop whereof was of gold, the sails of purple, and the oars of silver, which kept stroke in rowing after the sound of the music of flutes, howboys, citherns, viols, and such other instruments as they played upon the barge. And now for the person of herself: she was laid under a pavilion of cloth of gold of tissue, apparelled and attired like the goddess Venus commonly drawn in picture: and hard by her, on either hand of her, pretty fair boys apparelled as painters do set forth god Cupid, with little fans in their hands, with the which they fanned wind upon her. Her ladies and gentlewomen also, the fairest of them were apparelled like the nymphs Nereids (which are the mermaids of the waters) and like the Graces, some steering the helm, others tending the tackle and ropes of the barge, out of which there came a wonderful passing sweet savour of perfumes, that perfumed the wharf's side, pestered with innumerable multitudes of people. Some of them followed the barge all alongst the river-side: others also ran out of the city to see her coming in. So that in the end there ran such multitudes of people one after another to see her, that Antonius was left post alone in the market-place in his imperial seat to give audience: and there went a rumour in the people's mouths, that the goddess Venus was come to play with the god Bacchus, for the general good of all Asia.

SIR PHILIP SIDNEY
1554–86
An Apologie for Poetrie
(Originally written in 1580–1; published by Olney under this title in 1595)

Now therein of all Sciences . . . is our Poet the Monarch. For he doth not only show the way, but giveth so sweet a prospect into the way, as will entice any man to enter into it. Nay, he doth, as if your journey should lie through a fair Vineyard, at the first give you a cluster of Grapes, that full of that taste, you may long to pass further. He beginneth not with obscure definitions, which must blur the margent with interpretations, and load the memory with doubtfulness; but he cometh to you with words set in delightful proportion, either accompanied with, or prepared for, the well enchanting skill of Music; and with a tale forsooth he cometh unto you, with a tale which holdeth children from play, and old men from the chimney corner.

. . . .

So that sith the ever-praiseworthy Poesy is full of virtue-breeding delightfulness, and void of no gift that ought to be in the noble name of learning: sith the blames laid against it are either false or feeble; sith the cause why it is not esteemed in England is the fault of Poet-apes, not Poets; sith, lastly, our tongue is most fit to honour Poesy, and to be honoured by Poesy: I conjure you all that have had the evil luck to read this ink-wasting toy of mine, even in the name of the nine Muses, no more to scorn the sacred mysteries of Poesies, no more to laugh at the name of Poets, as though they were next inheritors to Fools, no more to jest at the reverent title of a Rhymer; but to believe, with *Aristotle,* that they were the ancient Treasurers of the Grecians' divinity; to believe, with *Bembus,* that they were first bringers in of all civility; to believe, with *Scaliger,* that no Philosopher's precepts can sooner make you an honest man than the reading of Virgil; to believe, with *Clauserus,* the translator of *Cornutus,* that it pleased the heavenly Deity, by *Hesiod* and *Homer,* under the veil of fables, to give us all knowledge, logic, rhetoric, philosophy, natural and moral, and *Quid non;* to believe, with me, that there are many mysteries contained in Poetry, which of purpose were written darkly, lest by profane wits it should be abused; to believe, with *Landin,* that they are so beloved of the Gods that whatsoever they write proceeds of a divine fury; lastly, to believe themselves, when they tell you they will make you immortal by their verses.

Thus doing, your name shall flourish in the Printers' shops; thus doing, you shall be of kin to many a poetical Preface; thus doing, you shall be most fair, most rich, most wise, most all; you shall dwell upon superlatives. Thus doing, though you be *Libertino patre natus,* you shall suddenly grow *Herculea proles, Si quid mea carmina possunt.* Thus doing, your soul shall be placed with *Dante's Beatrix,* or *Virgil's Anchises.* But if (fie of such a but) you be born so near the dull-making *Cataphract* of *Nilus* that you cannot hear the planet-like Music of Poetry, if you have so earth-creeping a mind that it cannot lift itself up to look to the sky of Poetry, or rather, by a certain rustical disdain, will become such a Mome as to be a *Momus* of Poetry; then, though I will not wish unto you the Ass's ears of *Midas,* nor to be driven by a Poet's verses (as *Bubonax* was) to hang himself, nor to be rhymed to death, as is said to be done in Ireland; yet thus much curse I must send you, in the behalf of all poets, that while you live, you live in love, and never get favour for lacking skill of a *Sonnet,* and, when you die, your memory die from the earth for want of an *Epitaph.*

JOHN LYLY
? 1554–1606

Euphues and his England
(First edition 1580)

IT happened that these English gentlemen conducted these
two strangers to a place, where divers gentlewomen were:
some courtiers, others of the country: where being welcome, they frequented almost every day for the space of
one month, entertaining of time in courtly pastimes,
though not in the court, insomuch that if they came not,
they were sent for, and so used as they had been country-
men, not strangers. *Philautus* with this continual access and
often conference with gentlewomen, began to wean himself from the counsel of *Euphues,* and to wed his eyes to the
comeliness of ladies, yet so warily as neither his friend
could by narrow watching discover it, neither did he by
any wanton countenance, bewray it, but carrying the image
of love engraven in the bottom of his heart, and the picture
of courtesy imprinted in his face, he was thought to *Euphues*
courtly, and known to himself comfortless. Among a
number of ladies he fixed his eyes upon one, whose countenance seemed to promise mercy, and threaten mischief,
intermeddling a desire of liking, with a disdain of love:
showing herself in courtesy to be familiar with all, and with
a certain comely pride to accept none, whose wit would
commonly taunt without despite, but not without disport,
as one that seemed to abhor love worse than lust, and lust
worse than murder, of greater beauty than birth, and yet
of less beauty than honesty, which got her more honour

16

by virtue than nature could by art, or fortune might by promotion. She was ready of answer, yet wary: shrill of speech, yet sweet: in all her passions so temperate, as in her greatest mirth none would think her wanton, neither in her deepest grief solemn, but always to look with so sober cheerfulness, as it was hardly thought whether she were more commended for her gravity of the aged, or for her courtliness of the youth: oftentimes delighted to hear discourses of love, but ever desirous to be instructed in learning: somewhat curious to keep her beauty, which made her comely, but more careful to increase her credit, which made her commendable: not adding the length of a hair to courtliness, that might detract the breadth of a hair from chastity: in all her talk so pleasant, in all her looks so amiable, so grave modesty joined with so witty mirth, that they that were entangled with her beauty, were enforced to prefer her wit before their wills: and they that loved her virtue, were compelled to prefer their affections before her wisdom: whose rare qualities caused so strange events, that the wise were allured to vanity, and the wantons to virtue, much like the river in *Arabia,* which turneth gold to dross, and dirt to silver. In conclusion, there wanted nothing in this English angel that nature might add for perfection, or fortune could give for wealth, or God doth commonly bestow on mortal creatures. And more easy it is in the description of so rare a personage, to imagine what she had not, than to repeat all she had. But such a one she was, as almost they all are that serve so noble a Prince, such virgins carry lights before such a *Vesta,* such Nymphs, arrows with such a *Diana.*

THOMAS NASHE
1567–1601

The Unfortunate Traveller
(First edition 1594)

A PRETTY round-faced wench was it, with black eyebrows, a high forehead, a little mouth, and a sharp nose, as fat and plum every part of her as a plover, a skin as sleek and soft as the back of a swan, it doth me good when I remember her. Like a bird she tripped on the ground, and bare out her belly as majestical as an ostrich. With a licorous rolling eye fixed piercing on the earth, and sometimes scornfully darted on the one side, she figured forth a high discontented disdain, much like a prince puffing and storming at the treason of some mighty subject fled lately out of his power. Her very countenance repiningly wrathful, and yet clear and unwrinkled, would have confirmed the clearness of her conscience to the austerest judge in the world. If in any thing she were culpable, it was in being too melancholy chaste and showing herself as covetous of her beauty as her husband was of his bags. Many are honest, because they know not how to be dishonest: she thought there was no pleasure in stolen bread, because there was no pleasure in an old man's bed. It is almost impossible that any woman should be excellently witty and not make the utmost penny of her beauty. This age and this country of ours admits of some miraculous exceptions, but former times are my constant informers. Those that have quick motions of wit have quick motions in every thing, iron only needs

18

many strokes, only iron wits are not won without a long siege of entreaty. Gold easily bends, the most ingenious minds are easiest moved, *Ingenium nobis molle Thalia dedit,* saith Sappho to Phao. Who hath no merciful mild mistress, I will maintain, hath no witty, but a clownish dull phlegmatic puppie to his mistress.

This magnifico's wife was a good loving soul, that had metal enough in her to make a good wit of, but being never removed from under her mother's and her husband's wing, it was not moulded and fashioned as it ought. Causeless distrust is able to drive deceit into a simple woman's head. I durst pawn the credit of a page, which is worth *ambs ace* at all times, that she was immaculate honest till she met with us in prison. Marry, what temptations she had then, when fire and flax were put together, conceit with yourselves but hold my master excusable. Alack he was too virtuous to make her vicious, he stood upon religion and conscience, what a heinous thing it was to subvert God's ordinance. This was all the injury he would offer her, sometimes he would imagine her in a melancholy humour to be his *Geraldine,* and court her in terms correspondent, nay he would swear she was his *Geraldine,* and take her white hand and wipe his eyes with it, as though the very touch of her might staunch his anguish. Now would he kneel and kiss the ground as holy ground which she vouchsafed to bless from barrenness by her steps. Who would have learned to write an excellent passion, might have been a perfect tragic poet, had he but attended half the extremity of his lament . . . .

My master beat the bush and kept a coil and a prattling,

but I caught the bird, simplicity and plainness shall carry it away in another world. God wot he was *Petro Desperato,* when I stepping to her with a dunstable tale made up my market. A holy requiem to their souls that think to woo a woman with riddles. I had some cunning plot you must suppose, to bring this about. Her husband had abused her, and it was very necessary she should be revenged: seldom do they prove patient martyrs who are punished unjustly, one way or other they will cry quittance whatsoever it cost them. No other apt means had this poor she, captived *Cicely,* to work her hoddypeak husband a proportionable plague for his jealousy, but to give his head his full loading of infamy. She thought she would make him complain for some thing, that now was so hard bound with an heretical opinion. How I dealt with her, guess gentle reader, *subaudi* that I was in prison, and she my silly jailer.

FRANCIS BACON, LORD VERULAM
1561–1626

Essays, or Counsels Civil and Moral
(First edition 1597; final form 1625)

ESSAY I: OF TRUTH

What is truth? said jesting Pilate, and would not stay for an answer. Certainly there be that delight in giddiness, and count it a bondage to fix a belief; affecting free-will in thinking, as well as in acting. And though the sects of philosophers of that kind be gone, yet there remain certain discoursing wits which are of the same veins, though there be not so much blood in them as was in those of the ancients. But it is not only the difficulty and labour which men take in finding out of truth, nor again that when it is found it imposeth upon men's thoughts, that doth bring lies in favour; but a natural though corrupt love of the lie itself. One of the later school of the Grecians examineth the matter, and is at a stand to think what should be in it, that men should love lies; where neither they make for pleasure, as with poets; nor for advantage, as with the merchant; but for the lie's sake. But I cannot tell: this same truth is a naked and open day-light, that doth not shew the masques and mummeries and triumphs of the world, half so stately and daintily as candlelights. Truth may perhaps come to the price of a pearl, that sheweth best by day; but it will not rise to the price of a diamond or carbuncle, that sheweth best in varied lights. A mixture of a lie doth ever add pleasure. Doth any man doubt, that if there were taken out of men's minds vain opinions, flattering hopes, false valuations, imaginations as one would, and the like, but it would leave the minds of a number of men poor shrunken things, full of melancholy and indisposition, and unpleasing to themselves? One of the fathers, in great severity, called poesy *vinum daemonum,* because it filleth the imagination, and yet it is but with the shadow of a lie. But it is not the lie that passeth through the mind, but the lie that sinketh in and settleth in it, that doth the hurt such as we spake of before. But howsoever these things are thus in men's depraved judgments and affections, yet truth, which only doth judge itself, teacheth that the inquiry of truth, which is the love-making or wooing of it, the knowledge of truth, which is the presence of it, and the belief of truth, which is the enjoying of it, is the sovereign good of human nature. The first creature of God, in the works of the days, was the light of the sense; the last was the light of reason; and his sabbath work, ever since, is the illumination of his Spirit. First he breathed light upon the face of the matter or chaos; then he breathed light into the face of man; and still he breatheth and inspireth light into the face of his chosen. The poet that beautified the sect that was otherwise inferior to the rest, saith yet excellently well: *It is a pleasure to stand upon the shore, and to see ships tost upon the sea: a pleasure to stand in the window of a castle, and to see a battle and the adventures thereof below: but no pleasure is comparable to the standing upon the vantage ground of truth* (a hill not to be commanded, and where the air is always clear and serene), *and to see the errors, and wanderings, and mists, and tempests, in the vale below:* so always that this prospect be with pity, and not with swelling or pride. Certainly, it is heaven upon earth, to have a man's mind move in charity, rest in providence, and turn upon the poles of truth.

AUTHORISED VERSION OF THE BIBLE

1611

The Book of Ecclesiastes

CHAPTER XI

CAST thy bread upon the waters: for thou shalt find it after many days. Give a portion to seven, and also to eight: for thou knowest not what evil shall be upon the earth. If the clouds be full of rain, they empty themselves upon the earth: and if the tree fall toward the south, or toward the north, in the place where the tree falleth, there it shall be. He that observeth the wind shall not sow; and he that regardeth the clouds shall not reap. As thou knowest not what is the way of the spirit, nor how the bones do grow in the womb of her that is with child: even so thou knowest not the works of God who maketh all. In the morning sow thy seed, and in the evening withhold not thine hand: for thou knowest not whether shall prosper, either this or that, or whether they both shall be alike good. Truly the light is sweet, and a pleasant thing it is for the eyes to behold the sun: But if a man live many years, and rejoice in them all; yet let him remember the days of darkness; for they shall be many. All that cometh is vanity. Rejoice, O young man, in thy youth; and let thy heart cheer thee in the days of thy youth, and walk in the ways of thine heart, and in the sight of thine eyes: but know thou, that for all these things God will bring thee into judgment. Therefore remove sorrow from thy heart, and put away evil from thy flesh: for childhood and youth are vanity.

CHAPTER XII, vv. 1–7

REMEMBER now thy Creator in the days of thy youth, while the evil days come not, nor the years draw nigh, when thou shalt say, I have no pleasure in them; While the sun, or the light, or the moon, or the stars, be not darkened, nor the clouds return after the rain: In the day when the keepers of the house shall tremble, and the strong men shall bow themselves, and the grinders cease because they are few, and those that look out of the windows be darkened, And the doors shall be shut in the streets, when the sound of the grinding is low, and he shall rise up at the voice of the bird, and all the daughters of musick shall be brought low; Also when they shall be afraid of that which is high, and fears shall be in the way, and the almond tree shall flourish, and the grasshopper shall be a burden, and desire shall fail: because man goeth to his long home, and the mourners go about the streets: Or ever the silver cord be loosed, or the golden bowl be broken, or the pitcher be broken at the fountain, or the wheel broken at the cistern. Then shall the dust return to the earth as it was: and the spirit shall return unto God who gave it.

THOMAS DEKKER
? 1570–1632

The Wonderful Year 1603
(First edition 1603)

WHAT an unmatchable torment were it for a man to be barred up every night in a vast silent Charnel-House? hung (to make it more hideous) with lamps dimly and slowly burning, in hollow and glimmering corners; where all the pavement should in stead of green rushes, be strewed with blasted Rosemary: withered Hyacinths, fatal Cypress and Yew, thickly mingled with heaps of dead men's bones: the bare ribs of a father that begat him, lying there: here the

24

Chapless hollow skull of a mother that bore him: round about him a thousand Corpses, some standing bolt upright in their knotted winding sheets: others half mouldered in rotten coffins, that should suddenly yawn wide open, filling his nostrils with noisome stench, and his eyes with the sight of nothing but crawling worms. And to keep such a poor wretch waking, he should hear no noise but of toads croaking, screech owls howling, mandrakes shrieking: were not this an infernal prison? would not the strongest-hearted man (beset with such a ghastly horror) look wild? and run mad? and die? And even such a formidable shape did the diseased City appear in: For he that durst (in the dead hour of gloomy midnight) have been so valiant, as to have walked through the still and melancholy streets, what think you should have been his music? Surely the loud groans of raving sick men, the struggling pangs of souls departing: In every house grief striking up an alarum: Servants crying out for masters: wives for husbands, parents for children, children for their mothers: here he should have met some franticly running to knock up sextons; there others fearfully sweating with coffins, to steal forth dead bodies, lest the fatal handwriting of death should seal up their doors. And to make this dismal consort more full, round about him Bells heavily tolling in one place, and ringing out in another: The dreadfulness of such an hour, is unutterable: let us go further.

If some poor man, suddenly starting out of a sweet and golden slumber, should behold his house flaming about his ears, all his family destroyed in their sleeps by the merciless fire, himself in the very midst of it, woefully and like a mad man calling for help: would not the misery of such a distressed soul, appear the greater, if the rich usurer dwelling next door to him, should not stir (though he felt part of the danger) but suffer him to perish, when the thrusting out of an arm might have saved him? how many thousands of wretched people have acted this poor man's part? how often hath the amazed husband waking, found the comfort of his bed lying breathless by his side! his children at the same instant gasping for life! and his servants mortally wounded at the heart by sickness! the distracted creature, beats at death doors, exclaims at windows, his cries are sharp enough to pierce heaven, but on earth no ear is opened to receive them.

JOHN DONNE
? 1572–1631

LXXX Sermons
(First edition 1640)

SERMON LXVI. 'THE SECOND OF MY PREBEND SERMONS UPON MY FIVE PSALMS.' ST PAUL'S. 29 JANUARY 1625-6

LET me wither and wear out mine age in a discomfortable, in an unwholesome, in a penurious prison, and so pay my debts with my bones, and recompense the wastefulness of my youth, with the beggary of mine age; Let me wither in a spittle under sharp, and foul, and infamous diseases, and so recompense the wantonness of my youth, with that loathsomeness in mine age; yet, if God withdraw not his spiritual blessings, his Grace, his Patience, If I can call my

suffering his Doing, my passion his Action, All this that is
temporal, is but a caterpillar got into one corner of my
garden, but a mildew fallen upon one acre of my Corn;
The body of all, the substance of all is safe, as long as the
soul is safe. But when I shall trust to that, which we call a
good spirit, and God shall deject, and empoverish, and
evacuate that spirit, when I shall rely upon a moral constancy, and God shall shake, and enfeeble, and enervate,
destroy and demolish that constancy; when I shall think
to refresh my self in the serenity and sweet air of a good
conscience, and God shall call up the damps and vapours
of hell itself, and spread a cloud of diffidence, and an
impenetrable crust of desperation upon my conscience;
when health shall fly from me, and I shall lay hold upon
riches to succour me, and comfort me in my sickness, and
riches shall fly from me, and I shall snatch after favour, and
good opinion, to comfort me in my poverty; when even
this good opinion shall leave me, and calumnies and mis-
informations shall prevail against me; when I shall need
peace, because there is none but thou, O Lord, that should
stand for me, and then shall find, that all the wounds that
I have, come from thy hand, all the arrows that stick in
me, from thy quiver; when I shall see, that because I have
given my self to my corrupt nature, thou hast changed
thine; and because I am all evil towards thee, therefore
thou hast given over being good towards me; when it
comes to this height, that the fever is not in the humours,
but in the spirits, that mine enemy is not an imaginary
enemy, fortune, not a transitory enemy, malice in great
persons, but a real, and an irresistible, and an inexorable,

and an everlasting enemy, The Lord of Hosts himself, The Almighty God himself, the Almighty God himself only knows the weight of this affliction, and except he put in that *pondus gloriae,* the exceeding weight of an eternal glory, with his own hand, into the other scale, we are weighed down, we are swallowed up, irreparably, irrevocably, irrecoverably, irremediably.

ROBERT BURTON
1577–1640

The Anatomy of Melancholy
(First edition 1621)

THE THIRD PARTITION: LOVE-MELANCHOLY
SECTION 2, MEM. III: SYMPTOMS OR SIGNS OF
LOVE-MELANCHOLY, IN BODY, MIND, GOOD, BAD, ETC.

... EVERY lover admires his mistress, though she be very deformed of herself, ill-favoured, wrinkled, pimpled, pale, red, yellow, tanned, tallow-faced, have a swollen juggler's platter face, or a thin, lean, chitty face, have clouds in her face, be crooked, dry, bald, goggle-eyed, blear-eyed, or with staring eyes, she looks like a squis'd cat, hold her head still awry, heavy, dull, hollow-eyed, black or yellow about the eyes, or squint-eyed, sparrow-mouthed, Persian hook-nosed, have a sharp fox-nose, a red nose, China flat, great nose, *nare simo patuloque,* a nose like a promontory, gubber-tushed, rotten teeth, black, uneven, brown teeth, beetle-browed, a witch's beard, her breath stink all over the room, her nose drop winter and summer, with a Bavarian poke under her chin, a sharp chin, lave-eared, with a long crane's neck, which stands awry too, *pendulis mammis,* 'her dugs like two double jugs', or else no dugs, in that other extreme, bloody-fallen fingers, she have filthy, long unpared nails, scabbed hands or wrists, a tanned skin, a rotten carcass, crooked back, she stoops, is lame, splay-footed, 'as slender in the middle as a cow in the waist', gouty legs, her ankles hang over her shoes, her feet stink, she breed lice, a mere changeling, a very monster, an oaf imperfect, her whole complexion savours, an harsh voice, incondite gesture, vile gait, a vast virago, or an ugly tit, a slug, a fat fustilugs, a truss, a long lean rawbone, a skeleton, a sneaker *(si qua latent meliora puta),* and to thy judgment looks like a mard in a lanthorn, whom thou couldst not fancy for a world, but hatest, loathest, and wouldest have spit in her face, or blow thy nose in her bosom, *remedium amoris* to another man, a dowdy, a slut, a scold, a nasty, rank, rammy, filthy, beastly quean, dishonest peradventure, obscene, base, beggarly, rude, foolish, untaught, peevish, Irus' daughter, Thersites' sister, Grobian's scholar; if he love her once, he admires her for all this, he takes no notice of any such errors or imperfections of body or mind,

> ... *Ipsa haec*
> *Delectant, veluti Balbinum polypus Agnae;*

he had rather have her than any woman in the world. If he were a king, she alone should be his queen, his empress. O that he had but the wealth and treasure of both the Indies to endow her with, a carrack of diamonds, a chain of pearl, a carcanet of jewels (a pair of calf-skin gloves of fourpence a pair were fitter), or some such toy, to send her for a token, she should have it with all his heart; he would spend myriads of crowns for her sake. Venus herself, Panthea, Cleopatra, Tarquin's Tanaquil, Herod's Mariamne, or Mary of Burgundy, if she were alive would not match her.

> (*Vincit vultus haec Tyndaridos,*
> *Qui moverunt horrida bella,*

let Paris himself be judge), renowned Helen comes short that Rhodopeian Phyllis, Larissaean Coronis, Babylonian Thisbe, Polyxena, Laura, Lesbia, etc., your counterfeit ladies were never so fair as she is.

> *Quicquid erit placidi, lepidi, grati, atque faceti,*
> *Vivida cunctorum retines Pandora deorum.*

Dicebam Triviae formam nihil esse Dianae, Diana was not to be compared to her, nor Juno, nor Minerva, nor any goddess. Thetis' feet were as bright as silver, the ankles of Hebe clearer than crystal, the arms of Aurora as ruddy as the rose, Juno's breasts as white as snow, Minerva wise, Venus fair; but what of this? Dainty come thou to me. She is all in all.

IZAAK WALTON
1593–1683

The Compleat Angler
(First edition 1653)

THE THIRD DAY: HOW TO FISH FOR, AND TO DRESS
THE CHAVENDER OR CHUB

PISCATOR. And now I will give you some rules how to catch [the chub]; and I am glad to enter you into the art of fishing by catching a chub, for there is no fish better to enter a young angler—he is so easily caught,—but then it must be in this particular way:

Go to the same hole in which I caught my chub, where in most hot days you will find a dozen or twenty chevens floating near the top of the water. Get two or three grass-hoppers as you go over the meadow, and get secretly behind the tree, and stand as free from motion as possible; then put a grasshopper on your hook, and let your hook hang a quarter of a yard short of the water, to which end you must rest your rod on some bough of the tree. But it is likely the chubs will sink down towards the bottom of the water at the first shadow of your rod (for a chub is the fearfullest of fishes), and will do so if but a bird flies over him and makes the least shadow on the water; but they will presently rise up to the top again, and there lie soaring till some shadow affrights them again. I say, when they lie upon the top of the water, look out the best chub; which you, setting yourself in a fit place, may very easily see, and move your rod, as softly as a snail moves, to that chub you intend to catch; let your bait fall gently upon the water three or four inches before him, and he will infallibly take the bait. And you will be as sure to catch him, for he is one of the leather-mouthed fishes, of which a hook doth scarce ever lose its hold; and therefore give him play enough before you offer to take him out of the water. Go your way presently, take my rod, and do as I bid you, and I will sit down and mend my tackling till you return back.

VENATOR. Truly, my loving master, you have offered me as fair as I could wish. I'll go and observe your directions.

Look you, master, what I have done: that which joys my heart, caught just such another chub as yours was.

PISCATOR. Marry, and I am glad of it: I am like to have a towardly scholar of you. I now see, that with advice and practice you will make an angler in a short time. Have but a love to it, and I'll warrant you.

VENATOR. But master! what if I could not have found a grasshopper?

PISCATOR. Then I may tell you, that a black snail, with his belly slit up, to show his white; or a piece of soft cheese, will usually do as well: nay sometimes a worm, or any kind of fly, as the ant-fly, the flesh-fly, or wall-fly; or the dor or beetle, which you may find under a cowturd; or a bob, which you will find in the same place, and in time will be a beetle; it is a short white worm, like to and bigger than a gentle, or a cod-worm, or a case-worm, any of these will do very well to fish in such a manner. And after this manner you may catch a trout in a hot evening:

when, as you walk by a brook, and shall see or hear him leap at flies, then, if you get a grasshopper, put it on your hook, with your line about two yards long, standing behind a bush or tree where his hole is, and make your bait stir up and down on the top of the water: you may, if you stand close, be sure of a bite, but not sure to catch him, for he is not a leather-mouthed fish: and after this manner you may fish for him with almost any kind of live fly, but especially with a grasshopper.

JEREMY TAYLOR

1613–67

The Rule and Exercises of Holy Dying

(First edition 1650–1)

CHAPTER I. A GENERAL PREPARATION TOWARDS A HOLY AND BLESSED DEATH, BY WAY OF CONSIDERATION

SECTION II

IT is a mighty change that is made by the death of every person, and it is visible to us who are alive. Reckon but from the spritefulness of youth, and the fair cheeks and full eyes of childhood, from the vigorousness, and strong flexure of the joints of five and twenty, to the hollowness and dead paleness, to the loathsomeness and horror of a three days' burial, and we shall perceive the distance to be very great, and very strange. But so have I seen a rose newly springing from the clefts of its hood, and at first it was fair as the morning, and full with the dew of heaven, as a lamb's fleece; but when a ruder breath had forced open its virgin modesty, and dismantled its too youthful and unripe retirements, it began to put on darkness, and to decline to softness, and the symptoms of a sickly age; it bowed the head, and broke its stalk, and at night having lost some of its leaves, and all its beauty, it fell into the portion of weeds and outworn faces: The same is the portion of every man, and every woman; the heritage of worms and serpents, rottenness and cold dishonour, and our beauty so changed that our acquaintance quickly knew us not, and that change mingled with so much horror, or else meets so with our fears and weak discoursings, that they who six hours ago tended upon us, either with charitable or ambitious services cannot without some regret stay in the room alone where the body lies stripped of its life and honour. I have read of a fair young German gentleman, who living, often refused to be pictured, but put off the importunity of his friends' desire, by giving way that after a few days' burial they might send a painter to his vault, and if they saw cause for it, draw the image of *his death unto the life*. They did so, and found his face half eaten, and his midriff and backbone full of serpents, and so he stands pictured among his armed ancestors. So does the fairest beauty change, and it will be as bad with you and me; and then, what servants shall we have to wait upon us in the grave, what friends to visit us, what officious people to cleanse away the moist and unwholesome cloud reflected upon our faces from the sides of the weeping vaults, which are the longest weepers for our funeral. . . .

CHAPTER III. SECTION VII

... [Death] is a thing that every one suffers, even persons of the lowest resolution, of the meanest virtue, of no breeding, of no discourse. Take away but the pomps of death, the disguises and solemn bug-bears, the tinsel, and the actings by candlelight, and proper and fantastic ceremonies, the minstrels and the noise-makers, the women and the weepers, the swoonings and the shriekings, the nurses and the physicians, the dark room and the ministers, the kindred and the watchers, and then to die is easy, ready and quitted from its troublesome circumstances. It is the same harmless thing that a poor shepherd suffered yesterday, or a maid servant to-day; and at the same time in which you die, in that very night, a thousand creatures die with you, some wise men, and many fools; and the wisdom of the first will not quit him, and the folly of the latter does not make him unable to die.

SIR THOMAS BROWNE
1605–82

Urn Burial
(First edition 1658)

CHAPTER V. SECTION IV

BUT the iniquity of oblivion blindly scattereth her poppy, and deals with the memory of men without distinction to merit of perpetuity. Who can but pity the founder of the pyramids? Herostratus lives that burned the Temple of Diana, he is almost lost that built it. Time hath spared the epitaph of Adrian's horse, confounded that of himself. In vain we compute our felicities by the advantage of our good names, since bad have equal durations; and Thersites is like to live as long as Agamemnon. Who knows whether the best of men be known? or whether there be not more remarkable persons forgot than any that stand remembered in the known account of time? Without the favour of the Everlasting Register, the first man had been as unknown as the last, and Methuselah's long life had been his only chronicle.

Oblivion is not to be hired: the greater part must be content to be as though they had not been, to be found in the Register of God, not in the record of man. Twenty-seven names make up the first story before the flood, and the recorded names ever since contain not one living century. The number of the dead long exceedeth all that shall live. The night of time far surpasseth the day, and who knows when was the equinox? Every hour adds unto that current arithmetic, which scarce stands one moment. And since death must be the Lucina of life, and even pagans could doubt whether thus to live, were to die; since our longest sun sets at right descensions, and makes but winter arches, and therefore it cannot be long before we lie down in darkness, and have our light in ashes; since the brother of death daily haunts us with dying mementos, and time that grows old in itself, bids us hope no long duration: diuturnity is a dream and folly of expectation.

Pious spirits who passed their days in raptures of futurity, made little more of this world, than the world that was before it, while they lay obscure in the chaos of preordination, and night of their fore-beings. And if any have been so happy as truly to understand Christian annihilation, extasis, exolution, liquefaction, transformation, the kiss of the Spouse, gustation of God, and ingression into the divine shadow, they have already had an handsome anticipation of heaven; the glory of the world is surely over, and the earth in ashes unto them.

To subsist in lasting monuments, to live in their productions, to exist in their names and predicament of chimeras, was large satisfaction unto old expectations, and made one part of their Elysiums. But all this is nothing in the metaphysics of true belief. To live indeed is to be again ourselves, which being not only an hope but an evidence in noble believers, 'tis all one to lie in St. Innocent's church-yard, as in the sands of Egypt. Ready to be anything, in the ecstasy of being ever, and as content with six foot as the *moles* of Adrianus.

JOHN MILTON

1608–74

Areopagitica

A speech for the Liberty of Unlicensed Printing

(First edition 1644)

NEXT, it is a lively and cheerful presage of our happy success and victory. For as in a body when the blood is fresh,

the spirits pure and vigorous, not only to vital, but to
rational faculties, and those in the acutest and the pertest
operations of wit and subtlety, it argues in what good plight
and constitution the body is; so when the cheerfulness of
the people is so sprightly up, as that it has not only wherewith to guard well its own freedom and safety, but to spare,
and to bestow upon the solidest and sublimest points of
controversy and new invention, it betokens us not de-
generated, nor drooping to a fatal decay, but casting off the
old and wrinkled skin of corruption to outlive these pangs,
and wax young again, entering the glorious ways of truth
and prosperous virtue, destined to become great and
honourable in these latter ages. Methinks I see in my mind
a noble and puissant nation rousing herself like a strong
man after sleep and shaking her invincible locks: methinks
I see her as an eagle mewing her mighty youth, and kind-
ling her undazzled eyes at the full midday beam, purging
and unscaling her long-abused sight at the fountain itself
of heavenly radiance; while the whole noise of timorous
and flocking birds, with those also that love the twilight,
flutter about, amazed at what she means, and in their
envious gabble would prognosticate a year of sects and
schisms.

What should ye do then, should ye suppress all this
flowery crop of knowledge and new light sprung up and
yet springing daily in this city? Should ye set an oligarchy
of twenty engrossers over it, to bring a famine upon our
minds again, when we shall know nothing but what is
measured to us by their bushel? Believe it, lords and commons! they who counsel you to such a suppressing, do as

good as bid ye suppress yourselves; and I will soon show how. If it be desired to know the immediate cause of all this free writing and free speaking, there cannot be assigned a truer than your own mild, and free, and humane government; it is the liberty, lords and commons, which your own valorous and happy counsels have purchased us; liberty which is the nurse of all great wits: this is that which hath rarefied and enlightened our spirits like the influence of heaven: this is that which hath enfranchised, enlarged, and lifted up our apprehensions degrees above themselves. Ye cannot make us now less capable, less knowing, less eagerly pursuing of the truth, unless ye first make yourselves, that made us so, less the lovers, less the founders of our true liberty. We can grow ignorant again, brutish, formal and slavish, as ye found us; but you then must first become that which ye cannot be, oppressive, arbitrary and tyrannous, as they were, from whom ye have freed us. That our hearts are now more capacious, our thoughts more erected to the search and expectation of greatest and exactest things, is the issue of your own virtue propagated in us; ye cannot suppress that unless ye reinforce an abrogated and merciless law, that fathers may dispatch at will their own children. And who shall then stick closest to ye and excite others? Not he who takes up arms for coat and conduct, and his four nobles of Danegelt. Although I dispraise not the defence of just immunities, yet love my peace better, if that were all. Give me the liberty to know, to utter, and to argue freely according to conscience, above all liberties.

EDWARD HYDE, EARL OF CLARENDON
1609–74

The History of the Rebellion and Civil Wars in England

(First published in 1702–4)

BOOK XII. 1649–50. THE DEATH OF MONTROSE

THAT he might not enjoy any ease or quiet during the short remainder of his life, their ministers came presently to insult over him with all the reproaches imaginable; pronounced his damnation; and assured him that the judgment he was the next day to suffer, was but an easy prologue to that which he was to undergo afterwards. After many such barbarities, they offered to intercede for him to the Kirk upon his repentance, and to pray with him; but he too well understood the form of their Common Prayer, in those cases, to be only the most virulent and insolent imprecations upon the persons of those they prayed against ... and therefore he desired them to spare their pains, and to leave him to his own devotions. He told them that they were a miserable, deluded, and deluding people; and would shortly bring that poor nation under the most insupportable servitude, ever people had submitted to. He told them he was prouder to have his head set upon the place it was appointed to be, than he could have been to have had his picture hang in the King's bed-chamber: that he was so far from being troubled that his four limbs were to be hanged in four cities of the kingdom, that he heartily wished that he had flesh enough to be

40

sent to every city in Christendom, as a testimony of the cause for which he suffered.

The next day, they executed every part and circumstance of that barbarous sentence, with the utmost inhumanity imaginable; and he bore it with all the courage and magnanimity, and the greatest piety, that a good Christian could manifest. He magnified the virtue, courage, and religion of the last King, exceedingly commended the justice, and goodness, and understanding of the present King; and prayed that they might not betray him, as they had done his father. When he had ended all he meant to say, and was expecting to expire, they had yet one scene more to act of their tyranny. The hangman brought the book that had been published of his truly heroic actions, whilst he had commanded in that kingdom, which book was tied in a small cord that was put about his neck. The marquis smiled at this new instance of their malice, and thanked them for it; and said he was pleased that it should be there; and was prouder of wearing it than ever he had been of the Garter; and so renewing some devout ejaculations, he patiently endured the last act of the executioner....

Thus died the gallant Marquis of Montrose, after he had given as great a testimony of loyalty, and courage, as a subject can do, and performed as wonderful actions in several battles, upon as great inequality of numbers, and as great disadvantages in respect of arms and other preparations for war, as have been performed in this age. He was a gentleman of a very ancient extraction, many of whose ancestors had exercised the highest charges under the King in that kingdom, and had been allied to the Crown itself. He was of very good parts, which were improved by a good education: he had always a great emulation, or rather a great contempt of the Marquis of Argyle (as he was too apt to contemn those he did not love) who wanted nothing but honesty and courage to be a very extraordinary man, having all other good talents in a very great degree. Montrose was in his nature fearless of danger, and never declined any enterprise for the difficulty of going through with it, but exceedingly affected those which seemed desperate to other men, and did believe somewhat to be in himself above other men, which made him live more easily towards those who were, or were willing to be, inferior to him (towards whom he exercised wonderful civility and generosity) than with his superiors or equals. He was naturally jealous, and suspected those who did not concur with him in the way, not to mean so well as he. He was not without vanity, but his virtues were much superior, and he well deserved to have his memory preserved, and celebrated amongst the most illustrious persons of the age in which he lived.

JOHN BUNYAN
1628–88

The Pilgrim's Progress
From this World to that which is to come Delivered under the Similitude of a Dream by John Bunyan.
(First edition 1678)

PART II

WHEN they had passed by this place, they came upon the borders of the Shadow of Death, and this valley was longer than the other; a place also most strangely haunted with evil things, as many are able to testify: but these women and children went the better through it, because they had daylight and because Mr Great-heart was their conductor.

When they were entered upon this valley, they thought that they heard a groaning as of dead men; a very great groaning. They thought also they did hear words of lamentation, spoken as of some in extreme torment. These things made the boys to quake: the women also looked pale and wan; but their guide bid them be of good comfort.

So they went on a little further, and they thought that they felt the ground begin to shake under them, as if some hollow place was there: they heard also a kind of hissing, as of serpents, but nothing as yet appeared. Then said the boys, Are we not yet at the end of this doleful place? But the guide also bid them be of good courage, and look well to their feet; lest haply, said he, you be taken in some snare.

Now James began to be sick; but I think the cause thereof was fear: so his mother gave him some of that glass of cordial that she had given her at the Interpreter's house, and three of the pills that Mr Skill had prepared, and the boy began to revive. Thus they went on till they came to about the middle of the valley; and then Christiana said, Methinks I see something yonder upon the road before us, a thing of a shape such as I have not seen. Then said Joseph, Mother, what is it? An ugly thing, child; an ugly thing, said she. But mother, what is it like? said he. 'Tis like I cannot tell what, said she; and now, it was but a little way off. Then said she, It is nigh.

Well, well, said Mr Great-heart, let them that are most afraid keep close to me. So the fiend came on, and the conductor met it; but when it was just come to him, it vanished to all their sights. Then remembered they what had been said some time ago, Resist the devil, and he will flee from you.

They went therefore on, as being a little refreshed. But they had not gone far before Mercy, looking behind her, saw, as she thought, something most like a lion, and it came a great padding pace after; and it had a hollow voice of roaring; and at every roar it gave, it made all the valley echo, and all their hearts to ache, save the heart of him that was their guide. So it came up, and Mr Great-heart went behind, and put the pilgrims all before him. The lion also came on apace, and Mr Great-heart addressed himself to give him battle. But when he saw that it was determined that resistance should be made, he also drew back, and came no further.

Then they went on again, and their conductor did go before them, till they came at a place where was cast up a pit the whole breadth of the way; and before they could be prepared to go over that, a great mist and a darkness fell upon them, so that they could not see. Then said the pilgrims, Alas! now what shall we do? But their guide made answer, Fear not, stand still, and see what an end will be put to this also: so they stayed there, because their path was marred. They then also thought that they did hear more apparently the noise and rushing of the enemies; the fire also, and the smoke of the pit, were much easier to be discerned. Then said Christiana to Mercy, Now I see what

my poor husband went through. I have heard much of
this place, but I never was here afore now. Poor man! he
went here all alone in the night; he had night also quite
through the way; also these fiends were busy about him,
as if they would have torn him in pieces. Many have spoke
of it; but none can tell what the Valley of the Shadow of
Death should mean till they come to it themselves. The
heart knows its own bitterness; and a stranger inter-
meddleth not with its joy. To be here is a fearful thing.

THOMAS TRAHERNE
? 1637–74

Centuries of Meditations

(MS. discovered and published for the first time in 1908)

THE THIRD CENTURY

WILL you see the infancy of this sublime and celestial
greatness? Those pure and virgin apprehensions I had from
the womb, and that divine light wherewith I was born are
the best unto this day, wherein I can see the Universe. By
the Gift of God they attended me into the world, and by
His special favour I remember them till now. Verily they
seem the greatest gifts His wisdom could bestow, for
without them all other gifts had been dead and vain. They
are unattainable by book, and therefore I will teach them
by experience. Pray for them earnestly: for they will make
you angelical, and wholly celestial. Certainly Adam in

Paradise had not more sweet and curious apprehensions of the world, than I when I was a child.

2

All appeared new, and strange at first, inexpressibly rare and delightful and beautiful. I was a little stranger, which at my entrance into the world was saluted and surrounded with innumerable joys. My knowledge was Divine. I knew by intuition those things which since my Apostasy, I collected again by the highest reason. My very ignorance was advantageous. I seemed as one brought into the Estate of Innocence. All things were spotless and pure and glorious: yea, and infinitely mine, and joyful and precious. I knew not that there were any sins, or complaints or laws. I dreamed not of poverties, contentions or vices. All tears and quarrels were hidden from mine eyes. Everything was at rest, free and immortal. I knew nothing of sickness or death or rents or exaction, either for tribute or bread. In the absence of these I was entertained like an Angel with the works of God in their splendour and glory, I saw all in the peace of Eden; Heaven and Earth did sing my Creator's praises, and could not make more melody to Adam, than to me. All Time was Eternity, and a perpetual Sabbath. Is it not strange, that an infant should be heir of the whole World, and see those mysteries which the books of the learned never unfold?

3

The corn was orient and immortal wheat, which never should be reaped, nor was ever sown. I thought it had stood from everlasting to everlasting. The dust and stones of the street were as precious as gold: the gates were at first the end of the world. The green trees when I saw them first through one of the gates transported and ravished me, their sweetness and unusual beauty made my heart to leap, and almost mad with ecstasy, they were such strange and wonderful things. The Men! O what venerable and reverend creatures did the aged seem! Immortal Cherubims! And young men glittering and sparkling Angels, and maids strange seraphic pieces of life and beauty! Boys and girls tumbling in the street, and playing, were moving jewels. I knew not that they were born or should die; But all things abided eternally as they were in their proper places. Eternity was manifest in the Light of the Day, and something infinite behind everything appeared: which talked with my expectation and moved my desire. The city seemed to stand in Eden, or to be built in Heaven. The streets were mine, the temple was mine, the people were mine, their clothes and gold and silver were mine, as much as their sparkling eyes, fair skins and ruddy faces. The skies were mine, and so were the sun and moon and stars, and all the World was mine; and I the only spectator and enjoyer of it. I knew no churlish proprieties, nor bounds, nor divisions: but all proprieties and divisions were mine: all treasures and the possessors of them. So that with much ado I was corrupted, and made to learn the dirty devices of this world. Which now I unlearn, and become, as it were, a little child again that I may enter into the Kingdom of God.

SAMUEL PEPYS
1633–1703

Diary

(First published in 1825; complete edition in 1893–6)

1669, 30TH APRIL

Up, and by coach to the coachmaker's; and there I do find
a great many ladies sitting in the body of a coach that must
be ended by to-morrow (they were my Lady Marquess of
Winchester, Bellasses, and other great ladies,) eating of
bread and butter, and drinking ale. I to my coach, which
is silvered over, but no varnish yet laid on, so I put it in a
way of doing; and myself about other business, and particularly to see Sir W. Coventry, with whom I talked a good
while to my great content: and so to other places, among
others, to my tailor's; and then to the beltmaker's, where
my belt cost me 55s. of the colour of my new suit; and here
understanding that the mistress of the house, an oldish
woman in a hat, hath some water good for the eyes, she
did dress me, making my eyes smart most horribly, and
did give me a little glass of it, which I will use, and hope
it will do me good. So to the cutler's, and there did give
Tom, who was with me all day, a sword cost me 12s. and a
belt of my own; and sent my own silver-hilt sword agilding
against to-morrow. This morning I did visit Mr Olden-
burgh, and did see the instrument for perspective made
by Dr Wren, of which I have one making by Browne; and
the sight of this do please me mightily. At noon my wife

came to me at my tailor's, and I sent her home, and myself and Tom dined at Hercules' Pillars; and so about our business again, and particularly to Lilly's, the varnisher, about my prints, whereof some of them are pasted upon the boards, and to my full content. Thence to the frame-maker's, one Norris, in Long Acre; who showed me several forms of frames, which were pretty, in little bits of mouldings to choose patterns by. This done, I to my coach-maker's, and there vexed to see nothing yet done to my coach, at three in the afternoon; but I set it in doing, and stood by till eight at night, and saw the painter varnish it, which is pretty to see how every doing it over do make it more and more yellow: and it dries as fast in the sun as it can be laid on almost; and most coaches are now-a-days done so, and it is very pretty when laid on well, and not too pale as some are, even to show the silver. Here I did make the workmen drink, and saw my coach cleaned and oiled; and staying among poor people there in the ally, did hear them call their fat child Punch, which pleased me mightily, that word being become a word of common use for all that is thick and short.

May 1. Up betimes. My wife extraordinary fine with her flowered tabby gown that she made two years ago, now laced exceeding pretty; and indeed was fine all over. And mighty earnest to go, though the day was very lowering; and she would have me put on my fine suit, which I did. And so anon we went alone through the town with our new liveries of serge, and the horses' manes and tails tied with red ribbons, and the standards thus gilt with varnish, and all clean, and green reins, that people did mightily look upon us; and the truth is, I did not see any coach more pretty, though more gay, than ours all the day; the day being unpleasing, though the Park full of coaches, but dusty, and windy, and cold, and now and then a little dribbling of rain; and what made it worse, there were so many hackney coaches as spoiled the sight of the gentle-men's; and so we had little pleasure.

JOHN AUBREY
1626–97

Brief Lives
(First published in 1813)

SIR JOHN DENHAM

Sir John Denham was unpolished with the smallpox; otherwise a fine complexion. He was of the tallest, but a little incurvetting at his shoulders, not very robust. His hair was but thin and flaxen, with a moist curl. His gait was slow, and was rather a stalking (he had long legs). His eye was a kind of light goose-grey, not big; but it had a strange piercingness, not as to shining and glory, but (like a Momus) when he conversed with you he looked into your very thoughts.

He was admitted of Trinity College in Oxford: I have heard Mr Josias Howe say that he was the dreamingest young fellow; he never expected such things from him as he has left the world. When he was there he would game extremely; when he had played away all his money he would play away his father's wrought rich gold caps. He was as good a student as any in the house. Was not suspected to be a wit.

He was much rooked by gamesters, and fell acquainted with that unsanctified crew, to his ruin. His father had some suspicion of it, and chid him severely, whereupon his son John (only child) wrote a little essay, *Against gaming, and to show the vanities and inconveniences of it,* which he presented to his father to let him know his detestation of it. But shortly after his father's death (who left 2000 or 1500 pounds in ready money, 2 houses well-furnished, and much plate) the money was played away first, and next the plate was sold. I remember about 1646 he lost 200 pound one night at New-cut.

He was generally temperate as to drinking, but one time when he was a student of Lincoln's Inn, having been merry at the tavern with his comrades late at night, a frolic came into his head, to get a plasterer's brush and a pot of ink and blot out all the signs between Temple Bar and Charing Cross, which made a strange confusion the next day, and 'twas in term time. But it happened that they were discovered, and it cost him and them some moneys. This I had from R. Estcott, Esq., that carried the ink pot.

At last, viz. 1640, his play of *The Sophy* came out, which did take extremely. Mr Edmund Waller said then of him, that he *broke out like the Irish Rebellion: three score thousand strong,* before anybody was aware.

At the beginning of the Civil War he was made governor of Farnham Castle for the king, but he was but a young soldier, and did not keep it. In 1643, after Edgehill fight, his poem called *Cowper's Hill* was printed at Oxford, in a sort of brown paper, for then they could get no better.

1647 he conveyed, or stole away, the two Dukes of York and Gloucester from St. James's, (from the tuition of the Earl of Northumberland) and conveyed them into France to the Prince of Wales and Queen Mother.

Anno 1652, he returned into England, and being in some straits was kindly entertained by the Earl of Pembroke at Wilton, where I had the honour to contract an acquaintance with him. He was, as I remember, a year with my lord of Pembroke at Wilton and London; he had then sold all the lands his father had left him. . . .

In the time of the Civil Wars, George Withers, the poet, begged Sir John Denham's estate at Egham of the Parliament, in whose cause he was a captain of horse. It happened that G. W. was taken prisoner, and was in danger of his life, having written severely against the king, etc. Sir John Denham went to the king, and desired his Majesty not to hang him, for that *whilst G. W. lived, he should not be the worst poet in England.*

JOHN DRYDEN
1631–1700

An Essay of Dramatick Poesy
(First edition 1668)

NEANDER SPEAKS

To begin, then, with Shakespeare. He was the man who of all modern, and perhaps ancient poets, had the largest and most comprehensive soul. All the images of nature were still present to him, and he drew them not laboriously but luckily: when he describes any thing, you more than see it, you feel it too. Those who accuse him to have wanted learning, give him the greater commendation: he was naturally learned; he needed not the spectacles of books to read nature; he looked inwards, and found her there. I cannot say he is every where alike; were he so, I should do him injury to compare him with the greatest of mankind. He is many times flat, insipid; his comic wit degenerating into clenches, his serious swelling into bombast. But he is always great, when some great occasion is presented to him; no man can say he ever had a fit subject for his wit, and did not then raise himself as high above the rest of poets,

Quantum lenta solent inter viburna cupressi.

The consideration of this made Mr Hales of Eton say, that there was no subject of which any poet ever writ, but he would produce it much better done in Shakespeare; and however others are now generally preferred before him, yet the age wherein he lived, which had contemporaries with him, Fletcher and Jonson, never equalled them to him in their esteem: and in the last king's court, when Ben's reputation was at highest, Sir John Suckling, and with him the greater part of the courtiers, set our Shakespeare far above him.

Beaumont and Fletcher, of whom I am next to speak, had, with the advantage of Shakespeare's wit, which was their precedent, great natural gifts, improved by study;

Beaumont especially being so accurate a judge of plays, that Ben Jonson, while he lived, submitted all his writings to his censure, and 'tis thought, used his judgment in correcting, if not contriving, all his plots. What value he had for him, appears by the verses he writ him; and therefore I need speak no farther of it. The first play that brought Fletcher and him in esteem was their PHILASTER: for before that, they had written two or three very unsuccessfully: as the like is reported of Ben Jonson, before he writ EVERY MAN IN HIS HUMOUR. Their plots were generally more regular than Shakespeare's, especially those which were made before Beaumont's death; and they understood and imitated the conversation of gentlemen much better; whose wild debaucheries, and quickness of wit in repartees, no poet before them could paint as they have done. Humour, which Ben Jonson derived from particular persons, they made it not their business to describe; they represented all the passions very lively, but above all, love. I am apt to believe the English language in them arrived to its highest perfection; what words have since been taken in, are rather superfluous than ornamental. Their plays are now the most pleasant and frequent entertainments of the stage; two of theirs being acted through the year for one of Shakespeare's or Jonson's: the reason is, because there is a certain gaiety in their comedies, and pathos in their more serious plays, which suits generally with all men's humours.

SAMUEL JOHNSON
1709–84

Lives of the Poets
(First edition 1779–81)

JOHN MILTON

THE plan of *Paradise Lost* has this inconvenience, that it comprises neither human actions nor human manners. The man and woman who act and suffer are in a state which no other man or woman can ever know. The reader finds no transaction in which he can be engaged; beholds no condition in which he can by any effort of imagination place himself; he has, therefore, little natural curiosity or sympathy.

We all, indeed, feel the effect of Adam's disobedience; we all sin like Adam and like him must bewail our offences; we have restless and insidious enemies in the fallen angels; and in the blessed spirits we have guardians and friends; in the Redemption of mankind we hope to be included; and in the description of Heaven and Hell we are surely interested, as we are all to reside hereafter either in regions of horror or of bliss.

But these truths are too important to be new; they have been taught to our infancy; they have mingled with our solitary thoughts and familiar conversations, and are habitually interwoven with the whole texture of life. Being therefore not new, they raise no unaccustomed emotion in the mind; what we knew before, we cannot learn; what is not unexpected, cannot surprise.

Of the ideas suggested by these awful scenes, from some

we recede with reverence, except when stated hours require their association; and from others we shrink with horror, or admit them only as salutary inflictions, as counterpoises to our interests and passions. Such images rather obstruct the career of fancy than incite it.

Pleasure and terror are indeed the genuine sources of poetry; but poetical pleasure must be such as human imagination can at least conceive; and poetical terror such as human strength and fortitude may combat. The good and evil of Eternity are too ponderous for the wings of wit; the mind sinks under them in passive helplessness, content with calm belief and humble adoration.

Known truths, however, may take a different appearance, and be conveyed to the mind by a new train of intermediate images. This Milton has undertaken, and performed with pregnancy and vigour of mind peculiar to himself. Whoever considers the few radical positions which the Scriptures afforded him, will wonder by what energetic operation he expanded them to such extent, and ramified them to so much variety, restrained as he was by religious reverence from licentiousness of fiction.

Here is a full display of the united force of study and genius; of a great accumulation of materials, with judgment to digest, and fancy to combine them: Milton was able to select from nature, or from story, from ancient fable, or from modern science, whatever could illustrate and adorn his thoughts. An accumulation of knowledge impregnated his mind, fermented by study, and exalted by imagination.

It has been therefore said, without an indecent hyperbole, by one of his encomiasts, that in reading *Paradise Lost* we read a book of universal knowledge.

But original deficiencies cannot be supplied. The want of human interest is always felt. *Paradise Lost* is one of the books which the reader admires and lays down, and forgets to take up again. None ever wished it longer than it is. Its perusal is a duty rather than a pleasure. We read Milton for instruction, retire harassed and overburdened, and look elsewhere for recreation; we desert our master, and seek for companions.

DANIEL DEFOE
? 1660–1731
The Life of Colonel Jack
(First edition 1722)

... [MY master] shared the money very honestly with me, only at the end he told me that though it was true he promised me half, yet as it was the first time and I had done nothing but look on, so he thought that it was very well if I took a little less than he did; so he divided the money, which was £12.10s, into two exact parts, viz. £6.5s. in each part, then he took £1.5s. from my part, and told me I should give him that for handsel. 'Well,' says I, 'take it then, for I think you deserve it all'; so, however, I took up the rest. 'And what shall I do with this now,' says I, 'for I have nowhere to put it?' 'Why, have you no pockets?' says he. 'Yes,' says I, 'but they are full of holes.' I have often thought since that, and with some mirth too, how I had really more wealth than I knew what to do with; for lodging I had none, nor any box or drawer to hide my money in, nor had I any pocket but such, as I say, was full of holes. I knew nobody in the world that I could go and desire them to lay it up for me; for, being a poor, naked, ragged boy, they would presently say I had robbed somebody, and perhaps lay hold of me, and my money would be my crime, as they say it often is in foreign countries. And now as I was full of wealth, behold it was full of care, for what to do to secure my money I could not tell, and this held me so long, and was so vexatious to me the next day, that I truly sat down and cried.

Nothing could be more perplexing than this money was to me all that night. I carried it in my hand a good while, for it was in gold all but 14s., and that is to say, it was in four guineas, and that 14s. was more difficult to carry than the four guineas. At last I sat down and pulled off one of my shoes and put the four guineas into that, but after I had gone a while my shoe hurt me so, I could not go, so I was fain to sit down again and take it out of my shoe and carry it in my hand. Then I found a dirty linen rag in the street, and I took that up, and wrapped it all together, and carried it in that a good way. I have often since heard people say, when they have been talking of money that they could not get in, 'I wish I had it in a foul clout.' In truth I had mine in a foul clout, for it was foul according to the letter of that saying, but it served me till I came to a convenient place, and then I sat down and washed the cloth in the kennel, and so then put my money in again.

Well, I carried it home with me to my lodging in the glass-house, and when I went to go to sleep, I knew not what to do with it. If I had let any of the black crew I was with know of it, I should have been smothered in the ashes for it, or robbed of it, or some trick or other put upon me for it. So I knew not what to do, but lay with it in my hand, and my hand in my bosom, but then sleep went from my eyes. Oh the weight of human care! I a poor beggar boy, could not sleep as soon as I had but a little money to keep, who before that could have slept upon a heap of brickbats or stones, cinders or anywhere, as sound as a rich man does on his down bed, and sounder too.

Every now and then dropping asleep, I would dream that my money was lost, and start like one frighted, then, finding it fast in my hand, try to go to sleep again, but could not for a long while; then drop and start again. At last a fancy came into my head that if I fell asleep, I should dream of the money, which if I should do, and one of the rogues should hear me, they would pick it out of my bosom, and of my hand too, without waking me, and after that thought I could not sleep a wink more; so that I passed that night over in care and anxiety enough, and this, I may safely say, was the first night's rest that I lost by the cares of this life, and the deceitfulness of riches.

JONATHAN SWIFT
1667–1745
A Tale of a Tub
(First edition 1704)

SECTION VII. A DIGRESSION IN PRAISE OF DIGRESSIONS

I HAVE sometimes heard of an Iliad in a Nut-shell; but it hath been my Fortune to have much oftener seen a Nut-shell in an Iliad. There is no doubt, that Human life has received most wonderful advantages from both; but to which of the two the world is chiefly indebted, I shall leave among the curious, as a problem worthy of their utmost enquiry. For the invention of the latter, I think the Commonwealth of Learning is chiefly obliged to the great modern improvement of Digressions: The late refinements in knowledge, running parallel to those of diet in our Nation, which among men of a judicious taste, are drest up in various compounds, consisting in Soups and Ollio's, Fricassées and Ragousts.

'Tis true, there is a sort of morose, detracting, ill-bred people, who pretend utterly to disrelish these polite innovations: And as to the similitude from diet, they allow the parallel, but are so bold to pronounce the example itself, a corruption and degeneracy of taste. They tell us, that the fashion of jumbling fifty things together in a dish, was at first introduced in compliance to a depraved and debauched appetite, as well as to a crazy constitution; And to see a man hunting thro' an Ollio, after the head and brains of a goose, a wigeon or a woodcock, is a sign, he wants a stomach and digestion for more substantial victuals. Farther, they affirm, that digressions in a book, are like the foreign troops in a state, which argue the nation to want a heart and hands of its own, and often, either subdue the natives, or drive them into the most unfruitful corners.

But, after all that can be objected by these supercilious censors; 'tis manifest, the Society of Writers would quickly be reduced to a very inconsiderable number, if men were put upon making books, with the fatal confinement of delivering nothing beyond what is to the purpose. 'Tis acknowledged, that were the case the same among us, as with the Greeks and Romans, when learning was in its cradle, to be reared and fed, and clothed by invention; it would be an easy task to fill up volumes upon particular occasions, without farther expatiating from the subject, than by moderate excursions, helping to advance or clear the main design. . . .

The whole course of things, being . . . entirely changed between us and the ancients; and the moderns wisely sensible of it, we of this Age have discovered a shorter, and more prudent method, to become scholars and wits, without the fatigue of reading or of thinking. The most accomplished way of using books at present, is twofold: Either first, to serve them as some men do lords, learn their titles exactly, and then brag of their acquaintance. Or secondly, which is indeed the choicer, the profounder, and politer method, to get a thorough insight into the index, by which the whole book is governed and turned, like fishes by the tail. For, to enter the palace of learning at the great gate, requires an expense of time and forms; therefore men of much haste and little ceremony, are content to get in by the back-door. For, the arts are all in a flying march, and therefore more easily subdued by attacking them in the rear. Thus Physicians discover the state of the whole body, by consulting only what comes from behind. Thus men catch knowledge by throwing their wit on the posteriors of a book, as boys do sparrows with flinging salt upon their tails. Thus human life is best understood by the wise man's rule of *regarding the end*. Thus are the sciences found like Hercules's oxen, by tracing them backwards. Thus are old sciences unravelled like old stockings, by beginning at the foot.

JOSEPH ADDISON

1672–1719

The Spectator, no 81. Saturday June 2nd, 1711

Qualis ubi audito venantum murmure tigris
Horruit in maculas... STATIUS

ABOUT the middle of last winter I went to see an opera at the theatre in the Haymarket, where I could not but take notice of two parties of very fine women, that had placed themselves in the opposite side boxes, and seemed drawn up in a kind of battle-array one against another. After a short survey of them, I found they were patched differently; the faces, on one hand, being spotted on the right side of the forehead, and those upon the other on the left. I quickly perceived that they cast hostile glances upon one another; and that their patches were placed in these different situations, as party-signals to distinguish friends from foes. In the middle boxes, between these two opposite bodies, were several ladies who patched indifferently on both sides of their faces, and seemed to sit there with no other intention than to see the opera. Upon inquiry I found that the body of Amazons on my right hand were Whigs, and those on my left, Tories; and that those who had placed themselves in the middle boxes were a neutral party, whose faces had not yet declared themselves. These last, however, as I afterwards found, diminished daily, and took their party with one side or the other; insomuch that I observed in several of them, the patches, which were before dispersed equally, are now all gone over to the Whig, or the Tory side of the face. The censorious say, that the men whose hearts are aimed at, are very often the occasions that one part of the face is thus dishonoured, and lies under a kind of disgrace, while the other is so much set off and adorned by the owner; and that the patches turn to the right or to the left, according to the principles of the man who is most in favour. But whatever may be the motives of a few fantastical coquettes, who do not patch for the public good so much as for their own private advantage, it is certain, that there are several women of honour who patch out of principle, and with an eye to the interest of their country. Nay, I am informed that some of them adhere so steadfastly to their party, and are so far from sacrificing their zeal for the public to their passions for any particular person, that in a late draught of marriage articles a lady has stipulated with her husband, that whatever his opinions are, she shall be at liberty to patch on which side she pleases.

I must here take notice, that Rosalinda, a famous Whig partisan, has most unfortunately a beautiful mole on the Tory part of her forehead; which being very conspicuous, has occasioned many mistakes, and given an handle to her enemies to misrepresent her face, as though it had revolted from the Whig interest. But, whatever this natural patch may seem to insinuate, it is well known that her notions of government are still the same. This unlucky mole, however, has misled several coxcombs; and like the hanging out of false colours, made some of them converse with Rosalinda in what they thought the spirit of her party, when on a sudden she has given them an unexpected fire, that has sunk them all at once. If Rosalinda is unfortunate in her mole, Nigranilla is as unhappy in a pimple, which forces her, against her inclinations, to patch on the Whig side.

I am told that many virtuous matrons, who formerly have been taught to believe that this artificial spotting of the face was unlawful, are now reconciled by a zeal for their cause, to what they could not be prompted by a concern for their beauty. This way of declaring war upon one another, puts me in mind of what is reported of the tigress, that several spots rise in her skin when she is angry, or, as Mr Cowley has imitated the verses that stand as the motto of this paper,

> . . . She swells with angry pride
> And calls forth all her spots on every side.

RICHARD STEELE
1672–1729
The Spectator, no 113. Tuesday July 10th, 1711

Haerent infixi pectore vultus. VIRGIL, *Aen.* IV, 4

IN my first description of the company in which I pass most of my time, it may be remembered that I mentioned

a great affliction which my friend Sir Roger had met with
in his youth; which was no less than a disappointment in
love. It happened this evening, that we fell into a very
pleasing walk at a distance from his house. As soon as we
came into it, 'It is,' quoth the good old man, looking
around him with a smile, 'very hard that any part of my
land should be settled upon one who has used me so ill
as the perverse widow did; and yet I am sure I could not
see a sprig of any bough of this whole walk of trees, but I
should reflect upon her and her severity. She has certainly
the finest hand of any woman in the world. You are to
know, this was the place wherein I used to muse upon her;
and by that custom I can never come into it but the same
tender sentiments revive in my mind, as if I had actually
walked with that beautiful creature under these shades.
I have been fool enough to carve her name on the bark
of several of these trees; so unhappy is the condition of
men in love, to attempt the removing of their passion by
the methods which serve only to imprint it deeper. She
has certainly the finest hand of any woman in the world.'

Here followed a profound silence, and I was not dis-
pleased to observe my friend falling so naturally into a
discourse which I had ever before taken notice he indus-
triously avoided. After a very long pause, he entered upon
an account of this great circumstance in his life, with an
air which I thought raised my idea of him above what I had
ever had before; and gave me the picture of that cheerful
mind of his, before it received that stroke which has ever
since affected his words and actions. But he went on as
follows:

'I came to my estate in my twenty-second year, and resolved to follow the steps of the most worthy of my ancestors who have inhabited this spot of earth before me, in all the methods of hospitality and good neighbourhood, for the sake of my fame; and in country sports and recreations for the sake of my health. In my twenty-third year I was obliged to serve as sheriff of the county; and in my servants, officers and whole equipage, indulged the pleasure of a young man (who did not think ill of his own person) in taking that public occasion of showing my figure and behaviour to advantage. You may easily imagine to yourself what appearance I made, who am pretty tall, ride well and was very well dressed, at the head of a whole county, with music before me, a feather in my hat, and my horse well bitted. I can assure you I was not a little pleased with the kind looks and glances I had from all the balconies and windows as I rode to the hall where the assizes were held. But, when I came there, a beautiful creature in a widow's habit sat in court to hear the event of a cause concerning her dower. This commanding creature (who was born for the destruction of all who behold her) put on such a resignation in her countenance, and bore the whispers of all around the court with such a pretty uneasiness, I warrant you, and then recovered herself from one eye to another, until she was perfectly confused by meeting something so wistful in all she encountered, that at last, with a murrain to her, she cast her bewitching eye upon me. I no sooner met it but I bowed like a great surprised booby; and knowing her cause to be the first which came on, I cried, like a captivated calf as I was, "Make way

66

for the defendant's witnesses". This sudden partiality made all the county immediately see the sheriff also was become a slave to the fine widow . . . .'

SAMUEL RICHARDSON
1689–1761

Clarissa Harlowe
(First edition 1747–8)

(Vol. III; Letter XXXIII—Mr Lovelace to John Belford, Esq. enclosing a Letter from Clarissa Harlowe to Mr Lovelace.)

A LETTER FROM CLARISSA HARLOWE TO MR LOVELACE

. . . I NEVER intended to write another line to you. I would not see you, if I could help it. O that I never had!

But tell me of a truth, is Miss Howe really and truly ill? Very ill? And is not her illness poison? And don't *you* know who gave it her?

What you, or Mrs Sinclair, or somebody (I cannot tell who) have done to my poor head, you best know: but I shall never be what I was. My head is gone. I have wept away all my brain, I believe; for I can weep no more. Indeed I have had my full share; so it is no matter.

But good now, Lovelace, don't set Mrs Sinclair upon me again. I never did her any harm. She *so* affrights me, when I see her! Ever since—when was it? I cannot tell. *You* can, I suppose. She may be a good woman, as far as I know. She was the wife of a man of honour—very likely—though forced to let lodgings for her livelihood. Poor gentlewoman! Let her know I pity her: but don't let her come near me again—pray don't!

Yet she may be a very good woman—

What would I say! I forget what I was going to say.

O Lovelace, you are Satan himself; or he helps you out in everything; and that's as bad!

But have you really and truly sold yourself to him? And for how long? What duration is your reign to have? Poor man! The contract *will* be out; and then what will be your fate!

O Lovelace! if you could be sorry for yourself, I would be sorry too—but when all my doors are fast, and nothing but the key-hole open, and the key of late put into that, to be where you are, in a manner without opening any of them—O wretched, wretched Clarissa Harlowe!

For I never will be Lovelace—let my uncle take it as he pleases.

Well, but now I remember what I was going to say. It is for *your* good—not *mine*—for nothing can do me good now! O thou villainous man! thou hated Lovelace!

But Mrs Sinclair may be a good woman. If you love me—but that you don't—but don't let her bluster up with her worse than mannish airs to me again! Oh, she is a frightful woman! If she *be* a woman! She needed not to put on that *fearful mask* to scare me out of my poor wits. But don't tell her what I say—I have no hatred to her—it is only fright, and foolish fear, that's all. She may not *be* a bad woman—but neither are all *men,* any more than all *women* alike. God forbid they should be like you!

Alas! you have killed my head among you—I don't say who did it! God forgive you all! But had it not been better to have put me out of all your ways at once? You might safely have done it! For nobody would require me at your hands—no, not a soul—except, indeed, Miss Howe would have said, when she should see you, What, Lovelace, have you done with Clarissa Harlowe? And then you could have given any slight gay answer—Sent her beyond sea; or, She has run away from me, as she did from her parents. And this would have been easily credited; for you know, Lovelace, she that could run away from *them,* might very well run away from *you.*

But this is nothing to what I wanted to say. Now I have it! I have lost it again—This foolish wench comes teasing me. For what purpose should I eat; for what end should I wish to live? I tell thee, Dorcas, I will neither eat nor drink. I cannot be worse than I am.

I will do as you'd have me—good Dorcas, look not upon me so fiercely—but thou canst not look so bad as I have seen somebody look.

Mr Lovelace, now that I remember what I took pen in hand to say let me hurry off my thoughts, lest I lose them again. Here I am sensible—and yet I am hardly sensible neither—but I know my head is not as it should be, for all that—therefore, let me propose one thing to you: it is for *your* good—not *mine:* and this is it:

I must needs be both a trouble and an expense to you. And here my Uncle Harlowe, when he knows how I am, will never wish any man to have me: no, not even *you,* who have been the occasion of it—barbarous and ungrateful! A less complicated villainy cost a Tarquin—but I forget what I would say again.

HENRY FIELDING
1707–54

The History of Tom Jones, a Foundling
(First edition 1749)

BOOK 18. CHAPTER XII

[TOM] caught [Sophia] in his arms, and kissed her with an ardour he had never ventured before. At this instant, Western, who had stood some time listening, burst into the room, and with his hunting voice and phrase, cried out, 'To her, boy! to her! go to her! That's it, little honeys! O, that's it! Well, what, is it all over? Has she appointed the day, boy? What, shall it be to-morrow or the next day? It shan't be put off a minute longer than next day, I am resolved'—'Let me beseech you, sir,' says Jones, 'don't let me be the occasion—'—'Beseech mine a—,' cried Western: 'I thought thou hadst been a lad of higher mettle than to give way to a parcel of maidenish tricks. I tell thee 'tis all flimflam. Zoodikers! she'd have the wedding tonight with all her heart. Wouldst not, Sophy? Come, confess, and be an honest girl for once. What, art dumb? why dost not speak?'—'Why should I confess, sir,' says Sophia, 'since it seems you are so well acquainted with my thoughts?'—'That's a good girl,' cries he; 'and dost consent then?'— 'No indeed, sir,' says Sophia. 'I have given no such consent'—'And wunt nut ha' un then to-morrow, nor next day?' says Western.—'Indeed, sir,' says she, 'I have no such intention.'—'But I can tell thee,' replied he, 'why hast nut; only because thou dost love to be disobedient, and to

plague and vex thy father'—'Pray sir—' said Jones, inter-
fering.—'I tell thee, thou art a puppy,' cries he. 'When I
vorbid her, than it was all nothing but sighing, and whin-
ing, and languishing, and writing: now I am vor thee, she
is against thee: all the spirit of contrary that's all. She is
above being guided and governed by her father; that is the
whole truth on't. It is only to disoblige and contradict
me.'—'What would my papa have me do?' cries Sophia.
'What would I ha' thee do?' says he, 'Why, gi' un thy hand
this moment.'—'Well, sir,' said Sophia, 'I will obey you.
There is my hand, Mr Jones'—'Well, and will you consent
to ha' un tomorrow morning?' says Western. 'I will be
obedient to you, sir,' cries she. 'Why then tomorrow
morning shall be the day,' cries he.—'Why then tomorrow
morning shall be the day, papa, since you will have it so,'
says Sophia. Jones then fell upon his knees and kissed her
hand in an agony of joy, while Western began to caper and
dance about the room, presently crying out, 'Where the
devil is Allworthy? He is without now, a-talking to that
d—d lawyer Dowling, when he should be minding other
matters'—He then sallied out in quest of him, and very
opportunely left the lovers to enjoy a few tender minutes
alone. But he soon returned with Allworthy, saying, 'If you
won't believe me, you may ask her yourself. Hast nut gin
thy consent, Sophy, to be married to-morrow?'—'Such are
your commands, sir,' cries Sophia; 'and I dare not be guilty
of disobedience'—'I hope, madam,' cries Allworthy, 'my
nephew will merit so much goodness, and will be always
as sensible as myself of the great honour you have done
my family. An alliance with so charming and so excellent

a young lady would indeed be an honour to the greatest in England'—'Yes,' cries Western, 'but if I had suffered her to stand shilly shally, dilly dally, you might not have had that honour yet awhile. I was forced to use a little fatherly authority to bring her to'—'I hope not, sir,' cries Allworthy: 'I hope there is not the least constraint'—'Why there,' cries Western, 'you may bid her unsay all again, if you will. Dost repent heartily of thy promise dost not, Sophy?'—'Indeed Papa,' cries she, 'I do not repent, nor do I believe I ever shall, of any promise in favour of Mr Jones'— 'Then, nephew,' cries Allworthy, 'I felicitate you most heartily; for I think you are the happiest of men. And madam, you will give me leave to congratulate you on this joyful occasion: indeed, I am convinced you have bestowed yourself on one, who will be sensible of your great merit, and who will at least use his best endeavours to deserve it'—'His best endeavours!' cries Western; 'that he will, I warrant un. Harkee, Allworthy. I'll bet thee five pounds to a crown we have a boy to-morrow nine months: but, prythee, tell me wut ha'. Wut ha' Burgundy, Champagne, or what? for please Jupiter, we'll make a night on't.'

TOBIAS SMOLLETT

1721–71

Peregrine Pickle

(First edition 1751)

CHAPTER II: COMMODORE TRUNNION

AT that instant, Mr Pickle's ears were saluted with such a strange noise, as even discomposed the muscles of his face, which gave immediate indications of alarm. This composition of notes at first resembled the crying of quails, and croaking of bull-frogs; but as it approached nearer, he could distinguish articulate sounds pronounced with great violence, in such a cadence as one would expect to hear from a human creature scolding thro' the organs of an ass. It was neither speaking nor braying, but a surprising mixture of both, employed in the utterance of terms absolutely unintelligible to our wondering merchant, who had just opened his mouth to express his curiosity, when the landlord, starting up at the well-known sound, cried 'Odd's niggers! there is the commodore with his company, as sure as I live;' and with his apron began to wipe the dust off an elbow chair placed at one side of the fire, and kept sacred for the ease and convenience of this infirm commander. While he was thus occupied, a voice still more uncouth than the former, bawled aloud, 'Ho! the house, ahoy!' Upon which the publican, clapping an hand to each side of his head, with his thumbs fixed on his ears, rebellowed in the same tone, which he had learned to imitate, 'Hilloah'. The voice again exclaimed, 'Have you got any attorneys aboard?' and when the landlord replied, 'No, no'; this man of strange expectation came in supported by his two dependants, and displayed a figure every way answerable to the oddity of his character.

He was in stature at least six feet high, tho' he had contracted an habit of stooping, by living so long on board; his complexion was tawny, and his aspect rendered hideous by a large scar across his nose, and a patch that covered the place of one eye. Being seated in his chair, with great formality the landlord complimented him upon his being able to come abroad again; and having, in a whisper, communicated the name of his fellow guest, whom the commodore already knew by report, went to prepare, with all imaginable dispatch, the first allowance of his favourite liquor, in three separate cans, (for each was accommodated with his portion apart) while the lieutenant sat down on the blind side of his commander; and Tom Pipes, knowing his distance, with great modesty took his station in the rear. After a pause of some minutes, the conversation was begun by this ferocious chief, who fixing his eye upon his lieutenant with a sternness of countenance not to be described, addressed him in these words: 'D—n my eyes! Hatchway, I always took you to be a better seaman than to overset our chaise in such fair weather. Blood! didn't I tell you we were running bump ashore, and bid you set in the lee-brace, and haul upon a wind?' 'Yes,' replied the other with an arch sneer, 'I do confess as how you did give such orders, after you had run us foul of a post, so as that the carriage lay along, and could not right herself.' 'I run you foul of a post!' cried the commander; 'd—n my heart! you're a pretty dog an't you, to tell me so above board to my face! Did I take charge of the chaise? Did I stand at the helm?' 'No,' answered Hatchway; 'I must confess you did not steer; but howsomever, you cunned all the way, and so, as you could not see how the land lay, being blind of your larboard eye, we were fast ashore, before you knew any-thing of the matter. Pipes, who stood abaft, can testify the truth of what I say.' 'D—n my limbs!' resumed the commo-dore, 'I don't value what you or Pipes say a rope yarn;

you're a couple of mutinous– I'll say no more; but, you shan't run your rig upon me, d—n ye, I am the man that learnt you, Jack Hatchway, to splice a rope, and raise a perpendicular.'

The lieutenant, who was perfectly well acquainted with the trim of his captain, did not choose to carry on the altercation any further; but, taking up his can, drank to the health of the stranger, who very courteously returned the compliment, without, however, presuming to join in the conversation, which then suffered a considerable pause.

LAURENCE STERNE
1713–68

The Life and Opinions of Tristram Shandy
(First edition 1760–7)

BOOK IV. CHAPTER XIII

I AM this month one whole year older than I was this time twelve-month; and having got, as you perceive, almost into the middle of my fourth volume—and no farther than to my first day's life—'tis demonstrative that I have three hundred and sixty-four days more life to write just now, than when I first set out; so that instead of advancing, as a common writer, in my work with what I have been doing at it—on the contrary, I am just thrown so many volumes back—was every day of my life to be as busy a day as this—And why not?—and the transactions and opinions of it to take up as much description—And for what reason should they be cut short? as at this rate I should just live 364 times faster than I should write—It must follow, an' please your worships, that the more I write, the more I shall have to write—and consequently, the more your worships read, the more your worships will have to read.

Will this be good for your worships' eyes?

It will do well for mine; and, was it not that my OPINIONS will be the death of me, I perceive I shall lead a fine life of it out of this self-same life of mine; or, in other words, shall lead a couple of fine lives together.

As for the proposal of twelve volumes a year, or a volume a month, it no way alters my prospect—write as I will, and rush as I may into the middle of things, as *Horace* advises—I shall never overtake myself whipp'd and driven to the last pinch; at the worst I shall have one day the start of my pen—and one day is enough for two volumes—and two volumes will be enough for one year.—

Heaven prosper the manufacturers of paper under this propitious reign, which is now opened to us—as I trust its providence will prosper every thing else in it that is taken in hand.—

As for the propagation of Geese—I give myself no concern—Nature is all bountiful—I shall never want tools to work with.

—So then, friend! you have got my father and my uncle *Toby* off the stairs, and seen them to bed?—And how did you manage it?—You dropp'd a curtain at the stair-foot—I thought you had no other way for it—Here's a crown for your trouble.

CHAPTER XIV

—Then reach me my breeches off the chair, said my father
to *Susannah.*—There is not a moment's time to dress you,
Sir, cried *Susannah*—the child's as black in the face as my—As
your what? said my father, for like all orators, he was a
dear searcher into comparisons.—Bless me, Sir, said
Susannah, the child's in a fit.—And where's Mr *Yorick?*—
Never where he should be, said *Susannah,* but his curate's in
the dressing room, with the child upon his arm, waiting
for the name—and my mistress bid me run as fast as I
could to know, as captain *Shandy* is the godfather, whether
it should not be called after him.

Were one sure, said my father to himself, scratching his
eye-brow, that the child was expiring, one might as well
compliment my brother *Toby* as not—and it would be a
pity, in such a case, to throw away so great a name as
Trismegistus upon him—but he may recover.

No, no,—said my father to *Susannah,* I'll get up—There
is no time, cried *Susannah,* the child's as black as my shoe.
Trismegistus, said my father—But stay—thou art a leaky
vessel, *Susannah,* added my father; canst thou carry *Trismegistus* in thy head, the length of the gallery without scat-
tering?—Can I? cried *Susannah,* shutting the door in a huff.
If she can, I'll be shot, said my father, bouncing out of bed
in the dark, and groping for his breeches.

Susannah ran with all speed along the gallery.

My father made all possible speed to find his breeches.

Susannah got the start, and kept it—'Tis *Tris*-something,
cried *Susannah*—There is no christian-name in the world,

said the curate, beginning with *Tris*—but *Tristram*. Then
'tis *Tristram-gistus,* quoth *Susannah*.

... There is no *gistus* to it, noodle!—'tis my own name,
replied the curate, dipping his hand, as he spoke, into the
bason—*Tristram!* said he, &c. &c. &c. &c., so *Tristram* was I
called, and *Tristram* shall I be to the day of my death.

JAMES BOSWELL
1740–95

Life of Samuel Johnson
(First edition 1791)

APRIL 7TH 1778

I TOLD him I had been present the day before, when Mrs
Montagu, the literary lady, sat to Miss Reynolds for her
picture; and that she said 'She had bound up Mr Gibbon's
History without the last two offensive chapters; for that
she thought the book so far good, as it gave, in an elegant
manner, the substance of the bad writers *medii aevi,* which
the late Lord Lyttleton advised her to read.' JOHNSON.
'Sir, she has not read them: she shows none of this im-
petuosity to me: she does not know Greek, and I fancy,
knows little Latin. She is willing you should think she
knows them; but she does not say she does.' BOSWELL.
'Mr Harris, who was present, agreed with her.' JOHNSON.
'Harris was laughing at her, Sir. Harris is a sound sullen
scholar; he does not like the interlopers. Harris, however,
is a prig, and a bad prig. I looked into his book, and thought

he did not understand his own system.' BOSWELL. 'He says plain things in a formal and abstract way, to be sure; but his method is good; for to have clear notions upon any subject, we must have recourse to analytic arrangement.' JOHNSON. 'Sir, it is what everybody does, whether they will or no. But sometimes things may be made darker by definition. I see a *cow*. I define her, *Animal quadrupes ruminans cornutum*. But a goat ruminates, and a cow may have no horns. *Cow* is plainer.' BOSWELL. 'I think Dr Franklin's definition of *Man* a good one.—"A tool-making animal."' JOHNSON. 'But many a man never made a tool: and suppose a man without arms, he could not make a tool.'

Talking of drinking wine, he said, 'I did not leave off wine because I could not bear it; I have drunk three bottles of port without being the worse for it. University College has witnessed this.' BOSWELL. 'Why, then, Sir, did you leave it off?' JOHNSON. 'Why, Sir, because it is so much better for a man to be sure that he is never to be intoxicated, never to lose the power over himself. I shall not begin to drink wine again till I grow old, and want it.' BOSWELL. 'I think, Sir, you once said to me, that not to drink wine was a great deduction from life.' JOHNSON. 'It is a diminution of pleasure to be sure; but I do not say a diminution of happiness. There is more happiness in being rational.' BOSWELL. 'But if we could have pleasure always, should not we be happy? The greatest part of men would compound for pleasure.' JOHNSON. 'Supposing we could have pleasure always, an intellectual man would not compound for it. The greatest part of men would compound, because the greatest part of men are gross.' BOS-

WELL. 'I allow there may be greater pleasures than from wine. I have had more pleasure from your conversation. I have indeed; I assure you I have.' JOHNSON. 'When we talk of pleasure, we mean sensual pleasure. When a man says he had pleasure with a woman, he does not mean conversation, but something of a different nature. Philosophers tell you that pleasure is *contrary* to happiness. Gross men prefer animal pleasure. So there are men who have preferred living among savages. Now, what a wretch must he be, who is content with such conversation as can be had among savages! You may remember an officer at Fort Augustus, who had served in America, told us of a woman whom they were obliged to *bind,* in order to get her back from the savage life.' BOSWELL. 'She must have been an animal, a beast.' JOHNSON. 'Sir, she was a speaking cat.'

HORACE WALPOLE, EARL OF ORFORD
1717–97
Letter to Lady Ossory

STRAWBERRY HILL, July 25th 1781

POOR human nature, what a contradiction it is! to-day it is all rheumatism and mortality, and sits with a death's head before it: to-morrow it is dancing! Oh! my lady, my lady, what will you say, when the next thing you hear of me after my last letter is, that I have danced three country dances with a whole set, forty years younger than myself! Shall you not think I have been chopped to shreds and boiled in Medea's kettle? Shall not you expect to see a print of Vestris teaching me?—and Lord Brudenell dying with envy? You may stare with all your expressive eyes, yet the fact is true. Danced—I do not absolutely say, *danced*—but I swam down three dances very gracefully, with the air that was so much in fashion after the battle of Oudenarde, and that was still taught when I was fifteen, and that I remember General Churchill practising before a glass in a gouty shoe.

To be sure you die with impatience to know the particulars. You must know then—for all my revels must out— I not only went five miles to Lady Aylesford's ball last Friday, but my nieces the Waldegraves, desired me there to let them come to me for a few days, as they had been disappointed about a visit they were to make at another place; but that is neither here nor there. Well, here they are, and last night we went to Lady Hertford at Ditton. Soon after, Lady North and her daughters arrived, and besides Lady Elizabeth and Lady Bel Conways, there were their brothers Hugh and George. All the *jeunesse* strolled about the garden. We ancients, with the Earl and Colonel Keene, retired from the dew into the drawing-room. Soon after the two youths and seven nymphs came in, and shut the door of the hall. In a moment we heard a burst of laughter, and thought we distinguished something like the scraping of a fiddle. My curiosity was raised, I opened the door and found four couples and a half standing up, and a miserable violin from the ale-house. Oh, said I, Lady Bel shall not want a partner; I threw away my stick, and *me voilà dansant comme un charme!* At the end of the third dance,

Lord North and his son, in boots, arrived. Come, said I, my lord, you may dance, if I have—but it ended in my *resigning my place* to his son.

Lady North has invited us for to-morrow, and I shall reserve the rest of my letter for the second volume of my regeneration; however, I declare I will not *dance*. I will not make myself too cheap; I should have the Prince of Wales sending for me three or four times a week to hops in Eastcheap. As it is, I feel I shall have some difficulty to return to my old dowagers, at the Duchess of Montrose's, and shall be humming the *Hempdressers* when they are scolding me for playing in flush.

Friday the 27th

I am not only a prophet, but have more command of my passions than such impetuous gentry as prophets are apt to have. We found the fiddles as I foretold; and yet I kept my resolution and did *not* dance, though the Syrens invited me, and though it would have shocked the dignity of old Tiffany Ellis, who would have thought it an indecorum. The two younger Norths and Sir Ralph Payne supplied my place. I played at cribbage with the matrons and we came away at midnight. So if I now and then do cut a colt's tooth, I have it drawn immediately. I do not know a paragraph of news—the nearer the minister, the farther from politics.

PS. My next jubilee dancing will be with Lady Gertrude.

EDWARD GIBBON

1737–94

The Decline and Fall of the Roman Empire

(First edition 1776, 1781, 1788)

CHAPTER XXI

A CHOSEN society of philosophers, men of a liberal education and curious disposition, might silently meditate, and temperately discuss in the gardens of Athens or the library of Alexandria, the abstruse questions of metaphysical science. The lofty speculations, which neither convinced the understanding, nor agitated the passions, of the Platonists themselves, were carelessly overlooked by the idle, the busy, and even, the studious part of mankind. But after the *Logos* had been revealed as the sacred object of the faith, the hope, and the religious worship of the Christians; the mysterious system was embraced by a numerous and increasing multitude in every province of the Roman world. Those persons who, from their age, their sex, or occupations, were the least qualified to judge, who were the least exercised in the habits of abstract reasoning, aspired to contemplate the economy of the Divine nature; and it is the boast of Tertullian, that a Christian mechanic could readily answer such questions as had perplexed the wisest of Grecian sages. Where the subject lies so far beyond our reach, the difference between the highest and the lowest of human understandings may indeed be calculated as infinitely small; yet the degree of weakness may perhaps by measured by the degree of obstinacy and dogmatic confidence. These speculations, instead of being treated as the amusement of a vacant hour, became the most serious business of the present, and the most useful preparation for a future, life. A theology, which it was incumbent to believe, which it was impious to doubt, and which it might be dangerous, and even fatal to mistake, became the familiar topic of private meditation and popular discourse. The cold indifference of philosophy was inflamed by the fervent spirit of devotion; and even the metaphors of common language suggested the fallacious prejudices of sense and experience. The Christians, who abhorred the gross and impure generation of the Greek mythology, were tempted to argue from the familiar analogy of the filial and paternal relations. The character of *Son* seemed to imply a perpetual subordination to the voluntary author of his existence; but as the act of generation, in the most spiritual and abstracted sense, must be supposed to transmit the properties of a common nature, they durst not presume to circumscribe the powers or the duration of the Son of an eternal and omnipotent Father . . . Their tender reverence for the memory of Christ, and their horror for the profane worship of any created being, would have engaged them to assert the equal and absolute Divinity of the *Logos,* if their rapid ascent towards the throne of Heaven had not been imperceptibly checked by the apprehension of violating the unity and sole supremacy of the great Father of Christ, and of the Universe. The suspense and fluctuation produced in the minds of Christians by those opposite tendencies, may be observed in the writings of the theologians who flourished after the end of the apostolic age, and before the origin of the Arian controversy. Their suffrage is claimed, with equal confidence, by the orthodox and by the heretical parties; and the most inquisitive critics have fairly allowed, that if they had the good fortune of possessing the catholic verity, they have delivered their conceptions in loose, inaccurate, and sometimes contradictory language.

EDMUND BURKE
1729–97

Reflections on the French Revolution
(First edition 1790)

IT is now sixteen or seventeen years since I saw the Queen of France, then the dauphiness, at Versailles; and surely never lighted on this orb, which she hardly seemed to touch, a more delightful vision. I saw her just above the horizon, decorating and cheering the elevated sphere she just began to move in,—glittering like the morning star, full of life, and splendour, and joy. Oh! what a revolution! and what an heart must I have, to contemplate without emotion that elevation and that fall! Little did I dream when she added titles of veneration to those of enthusiastic, distant, respectful love, that she should ever be obliged to carry the sharp antidote against disgrace concealed in that bosom; little did I dream that I should have lived to see such disasters fallen upon her in a nation of gallant men, in a nation of men of honour, and of cavaliers.

I thought ten thousand swords must have leaped from their scabbards to avenge even a look that threatened her with insult. But the age of chivalry is gone. That of sophisters, economists, and calculators, has succeeded; and the glory of Europe is extinguished for ever. Never, never more, shall we behold that generous loyalty to rank and sex, that proud submission, that dignified obedience, that subordination of the heart, which kept alive, even in servitude itself, the spirit of an exalted freedom. The unbought grace of life, the cheap defence of nations, the nurse of manly sentiment, and heroic enterprise is gone! It is gone, that sensibility of principle, that chastity of honour, which felt a stain like a wound, which inspired courage while it mitigated ferocity, which ennobled whatever it touched, and under which vice itself lost half its evil, by losing all its grossness.

This mixed system of opinion and sentiment had its origin in the ancient chivalry; and the principle, though varied in its appearance by the varying state of human affairs, subsisted and influenced through a long succession of generations, even to the time we live in. If it should ever be totally extinguished, the loss I fear will be great. . . . It is this which has distinguished it under all its forms of government, and distinguished it to its advantage, from the states of Asia, and possibly from those states which flourished in the most brilliant periods of the antique world. It was this, which, without confounding ranks, had produced a noble equality, and handed it down through all the gradations of social life. It was this opinion which mitigated kings into companions, and raised private men to be fellows with kings. Without force, or opposition, it subdued the fierceness of pride and power, it obliged sovereigns to submit to the soft collar of social esteem, compelled stern authority to submit to elegance, and gave a dominating vanquisher of laws, to be subdued by manners.

But now all is changed. All the pleasing illusions, which made power gentle, and obedience liberal, which harmonized the different shades of life, and which, by a bland assimilation, incorporated into politics the sentiments which beautify and soften private society, are to be dissolved by this new conquering empire of light and reason. All the decent drapery of life is to be rudely torn off. All the superadded ideas, furnished from the wardrobe of a moral imagination, which the heart owns, and the understanding ratifies, as necessary to cover the defects of our naked, shivering nature, and to raise it to dignity in our own estimation are to be exploded as a ridiculous, absurd, and antiquated fashion.

JANE AUSTEN
1775–1817

Emma
(First edition 1816)

CHAPTER XXII

HUMAN nature is so well disposed towards those who are in interesting situations, that a young person who either marries or dies is sure of being kindly spoken of.

A week had not passed since Miss Hawkins's name was

first mentioned in Highbury before she was, by some means or other, discovered to have every recommendation of person and mind,—to be handsome, elegant, highly accomplished, and perfectly amiable; and when Mr Elton himself arrived to triumph in his happy prospects, and circulate the fame of her merits, there was very little more for him to do than to tell her Christian name, and say whose music she principally played.

Mr Elton returned, a very happy man. He had gone away rejected and mortified, disappointed in a very sanguine hope, after a series of what had appeared to him strong encouragement; and not only losing the right lady, but finding himself debased to the level of a very wrong one. He had gone away deeply offended; he came back engaged to another, and to another as superior, of course, to the first, as under such circumstances what is gained always is to what is lost. He came back gay and self-satisfied, eager and busy, caring nothing for Miss Woodhouse, and defying Miss Smith.

The charming Augusta Hawkins, in addition to all the usual advantages of perfect beauty and merit, was in possession of an independent fortune, of so many thousands as would always be called ten,—a point of some dignity, as well as some convenience. The story told well; he had not thrown himself away—he had gained a woman of £10,000 or thereabouts, and he had gained her with such delightful rapidity; the first hour of introduction had been so very soon followed by distinguishing notice; the history which he had to give Mrs Cole of the rise and progress of the affair was so glorious; the steps so quick, from the accidental rencontre to the dinner at Mr Green's, and the party at Mrs Brown's—smiles and blushes rising in importance,—with consciousness and agitation richly scattered; the lady had been so easily impressed,—so sweetly disposed;—had, in short, to use a most intelligible phrase, been so very ready to have him, that vanity and prudence were equally contented.

He had caught both substance and shadow, both fortune and affection, and was just the happy man he ought to be;—talking only of himself and his own concerns,—expecting to be congratulated,—ready to be laughed at,—and with cordial, fearless smiles, now addressing all the young ladies of the place, to whom, a few weeks ago, he would have been more cautiously gallant.

The wedding was no distant event, as the parties had only themselves to please, and nothing but the necessary preparations to wait for; and when he set out for Bath again, there was a general expectation, which a certain glance of Mrs Cole's did not seem to contradict, that when he next entered Highbury he would bring his bride.

During his present short stay, Emma had barely seen him; but just enough to feel that the first meeting was over, and to give her the impression of his not being improved by the mixture of pique and pretension now spread over his air. She was, in fact, beginning very much to wonder that she had ever thought him pleasing at all; and his sight was so inseparably connected with some very disagreeable feelings that, except in a moral light—as a penance, a lesson, a source of profitable humiliation to her own mind—she would have been thankful to be assured of never seeing him again. She wished him very well; but he gave her pain; and his welfare twenty miles off would administer most satisfaction.

SIR WALTER SCOTT
1771–1832

The Heart of Mid-Lothian
(First edition 1818)

CHAPTER VII

THE rioters... continued to act with the same air of deliberate confidence and security which had marked all their proceedings. When the object of their resentment dropped one of his slippers, they stopped, sought for it, and replaced it upon his foot with great deliberation. As they descended the Bow towards the fatal spot where they designed to complete their purpose, it was suggested that there should be a rope kept in readiness. For this purpose, the booth of a man who dealt in cordage was forced open, a coil of rope fit for their purpose was selected to serve as a halter, and the dealer next morning found that a guinea had been left on his counter in exchange; so anxious were the perpetrators of this daring action to show that they meditated not the slightest wrong or infraction of law, excepting so far as Porteous was himself concerned.

Leading, or carrying along with them, in this determined and regular manner, the object of their vengeance, they at length reached the place of common execution, the scene of his crime, and destined spot of his sufferings. Several of the rioters (if they should not rather be described as conspirators) endeavoured to remove the stone which filled up the socket in which the end of the fatal tree was sunk when it was erected for its fatal purpose; others sought for the means of constructing a temporary gibbet, the place in which the gallows itself was deposited being reported too secure to be forced, without much loss of time. Butler endeavoured to avail himself of the delay afforded by these circumstances, to turn the people from their desperate design. 'For God's sake,' he exclaimed, 'remember it is the image of your Creator which you are about to deface in the person of this unfortunate man! Wretched as he is, and wicked as he may be, he has a share in every promise of Scripture, and you cannot destroy him in impenitence without blotting his name from the Book of Life—Do not destroy soul and body; give time for preparation.'

'What time had they', returned a stern voice, 'whom he murdered on this very spot?—The laws both of God and man call for his death.'

'But what, my friends,' insisted Butler, with a generous disregard to his own safety—'what hath constituted you his judges?'

'We are not his judges,' replied the same person; 'he has been already judged and condemned by lawful authority. We are those whom Heaven, and our righteous anger, has stirred up to execute judgment, when a corrupt government would have protected a murderer.'

'I am none', said the unfortunate Porteous; 'that which

you charge upon me fell out in self-defence, in the lawful exercise of my duty.'

'Away with him—away with him!' was the general cry. 'Why do you trifle away time in making a gallows?—that dyester's pole is good enough for the homicide.'

The unhappy man was forced to his fate with remorseless rapidity. Butler separated from him by the press, escaped the last horrors of his struggles. Unnoticed by those who had hitherto detained him as a prisoner, he fled from the fatal spot, without much caring in what direction his course lay. A loud shout proclaimed the stern delight with which the agents of this deed regarded its completion. Butler, then, at the opening into the low street called the Cowgate, cast back a terrified glance, and, by the red and dusky light of the torches, he could discern a figure wavering and struggling as it hung suspended above the heads of the multitude, and could even observe men striking at it with their Lochaber-axes and partisans. The sight was of a nature to double his horror, and to add wings to his flight.

WILLIAM HAZLITT
1778–1830

The Plain Speaker, April 1823

MY FIRST ACQUAINTANCE WITH POETS

THE next day Wordsworth arrived from Bristol at Coleridge's cottage. I think I see him now. He answered in some degree to his friend's description of him, but was more gaunt and Don Quixote-like. He was quaintly dressed (according to the *costume* of that unconstrained period) in a brown fustian jacket and striped pantaloons. There was something of a roll, a lounge in his gait, not unlike his own *Peter Bell*. There was a severe, worn pressure of thought about his temples, a fire in his eye (as if he saw something in objects more than the outward appearance), an intense, high, narrow, forehead, a Roman nose, cheeks furrowed by strong purpose and feeling, and a convulsive inclination to laughter about the mouth, a good deal at variance with the solemn, stately expression of the rest of his face. Chantrey's bust wants the marking traits; but he was teazed into making it regular and heavy: Haydon's head of him, introduced into the *Entrance of Christ into Jerusalem,* is the most like his drooping weight of thought and expression. He sat down and talked very naturally and freely, with a mixture of clear, gushing accents in his voice, a deep guttural intonation, and a strong tincture of the northern *burr,* like the crust on wine. He instantly began to make havoc of the half of a Cheshire cheese on the table, and said, triumphantly, that 'his marriage with experience had not been so productive as Mr Southey's in teaching him a knowledge of the good things of this life'. He had been to see the *Castle Spectre* by Monk Lewis, while at Bristol, and described it very well. He said 'it fitted the taste of the audience like a glove'. This *ad captandum* merit was however by no means a recommendation of it, according to the severe principles of the new school, which reject rather than court popular effect. Wordsworth, looking out of the low, latticed window, said 'How beautifully the sun sets on that yellow bank!' I thought within myself, 'With what eyes these poets see nature!' and ever after, when I saw the sun-set stream upon the objects facing it, conceived I had made a discovery, or thanked Mr Wordsworth for having made one for me! We went over to All-Foxden again the day following, and Wordsworth read us the story of *Peter Bell* in the open air; and the comment made upon it by his face and voice was very different from that of some later critics! Whatever might be thought of the poem, 'his face was as a book where men might read strange matters', and he announced the fate of his hero in prophetic tones. There is a *chaunt* in the recitation both of Coleridge and Wordsworth, which acts as a spell upon the hearer, and disarms the judgment. Perhaps they have deceived themselves by making habitual use of this ambiguous accompaniment. Coleridge's manner is more full, animated, and varied; Wordsworth's more equable, sustained, and internal. The one might be termed more *dramatic,* the other more *lyrical.* Coleridge has told me that he himself liked to compose in walking over uneven ground, or breaking through the straggling branches of a copse-wood; whereas Wordsworth always wrote (if he could) walking up and down a straight gravel-walk, or in some spot where the continuity of his verse met with no collateral interruption. Returning that same evening, I got into a metaphysical argument with Wordsworth, while Coleridge was explaining the different notes of the nightingale to his sister, in which we neither of us succeeded in making ourselves perfectly clear and intelligible. Thus I passed three weeks at Nether Stowey and in the neighbourhood, generally devoting the afternoons to a delightful chat in an arbour made of bark by the poet's friend Tom Poole, sitting under two fine elm-trees, and listening to the bees humming round us, while we quaffed our flip.

SAMUEL TAYLOR COLERIDGE
1772–1834

Biographia Literaria
(First edition 1817)

CHAPTER XIV: OCCASION OF THE LYRICAL BALLADS

DURING the first year that Mr Wordsworth and I were neighbours, our conversations turned frequently on the two cardinal points of poetry, the power of exciting the sympathy of the reader by a faithful adherence to the truth of nature, and the power of giving the interest of novelty by the modifying colours of imagination. The sudden charm, which accidents of light and shade, which moonlight or sunset diffused over a known and familiar landscape, appeared to represent the practicability of combining both. These are the poetry of nature. The thought suggested itself—(to which of us I do not recollect)—that a series of poems might be composed of two sorts. In the one, the incidents and agents were to be, in part at least, supernatural; and the excellence aimed at was to consist in the interesting of the affections by the dramatic truth of such emotions, as would naturally accompany such situations, supposing them real. And real in this sense they have been to every human being who, from whatever source of delusion, has at any time believed himself under supernatural agency. For the second class, subjects were to be chosen from ordinary life; the characters and incidents were to be such as will be found in every village and its vicinity, where there is a meditative and feeling mind to seek after them, or to notice them, when they present themselves.

In this idea originated the plan of the LYRICAL BALLADS: in which it was agreed, that my endeavours should be directed to persons and characters supernatural, or at least romantic; yet so as to transfer from our inward nature a human interest and a semblance of truth sufficient to procure for these shadows of imagination that willing suspension of disbelief for the moment, which constitutes poetic faith. Mr Wordsworth, on the other hand, was to propose to himself as his object, to give the charm of novelty to things of every day, and to excite a feeling analogous to the supernatural, by awakening the mind's attention to the lethargy of custom, and directing it to the loveliness and the wonders of the world before us; an inexhaustible treasure, but for which, in consequence of the film of familiarity and selfish solicitude, we have eyes, yet see not, ears that hear not, and hearts that neither feel nor understand.

. . . .

The poet, described in ideal perfection, brings the whole soul of man into activity, with the subordination of its faculties to each other according to their relative worth and dignity. He diffuses a tone and spirit of unity, that blends and (as it were) *fuses,* each into each, by that synthetic and magical power, to which I would exclusively appropriate the name of Imagination. This power, first put into action by the will and understanding, and retained under their irremissive, though gentle and unnoticed, control, *laxis effertur habenis*, reveals itself in the balance or reconcilement of opposite or discordant qualities: of sameness, with difference; of the general with the concrete; the idea with the image; the individual with the representative; the sense of novelty and freshness with old and familiar objects; a more than usual state of emotion with more than usual order; judgment ever awake and steady self-possession with enthusiasm and feeling profound or vehement; and while it blends and harmonizes the natural and the artificial, still subordinates art to nature; the manner to the matter; and our admiration of the poet to our sympathy with the poetry.

JOHN KEATS
1795–1821

Letter to Richard Woodhouse

Tuesday, October 27, 1818

My dear Woodhouse

Your letter gave me a great satisfaction; more on account of its friendliness, than any relish of that matter in it which is accounted so acceptable in the 'genus irritabile'. The best answer I can give you is in a clerk-like manner to make some observations on two principle points, which seem to point like indices into the midst of the whole pro and con, about genius, and views and atchievements and ambition and coetera. 1st. As to the poetical Character itself (I mean that sort of which, if I am any thing, I am a Member; that sort distinguished from the wordsworthian or egotistical sublime; which is a thing per se and stands alone) it is not itself—it has no self—it is every thing and nothing—It has no character—it enjoys light and shade; it lives in gusto, be it foul or fair, high or low, rich or poor, mean or elevated —It has as much delight in conceiving an Iago as an Imogen. What shocks the virtuous philosopher, delights the ca- melion Poet. It does no harm from its relish of the dark side of things any more than from its taste for the bright one; because they both end in speculation. A Poet is the most unpoetical of any thing in existence; because he has no Identity—he is continually infor[ming] and filling some other Body—The Sun, the Moon, the Sea and Men and Women who are creatures of impulse are poetical and have about them an unchangeable attribute—the poet has none; no identity—he is certainly the most unpoetical of all God's Creatures. If then he has no self, and if I am a Poet, where is the Wonder that I should say I would write no more? Might I not at that very instant have been cogitating on the Characters of Saturn and Ops? It is a wretched thing to confess; but is a very fact that not one word I ever utter can be taken for granted as an opinion growing out of my identical nature—how can it, when I have no nature? When I am in a room with People if I ever am free from specu- lating on creations of my own brain, then not myself goes home to myself: but the identity of every one in the room begins to press upon me that I am in a very little time an[ni]hilated—not only among Men; it would be the same in a Nursery of children: I know not whether I make myself wholly understood: I hope enough so to let you see that no dependence is to be placed on what I said that day.

In the second place I will speak of my views, and of the life I purpose to myself. I am ambitious of doing the world some good: if I should be spared that may be the work of maturer years—in the interval I will assay to reach to as high a summit in Poetry as the nerve bestowed upon me will suffer. The faint conceptions I have of Poems to come brings the blood frequently into my forehead. All I hope is that I may not lose all interest in human affairs—that the solitary indifference I feel for applause even from the finest spirits, will not blunt any acuteness of vision I may have. I do not think it will.—I feel assured I should write from the mere yearning and fondness I have for the Beautiful even if my night's labours should be burnt every morning, and no eye ever shine upon them. But even now I am perhaps not speaking from myself: but from some character in whose soul I now live. I am sure however that this next sentence is from myself. I feel your anxiety, good opinion and friendliness in the highest degree, and am

Your's most sincerely

JOHN KEATS

43196

CHARLES LAMB
1775–1834

Essays of Elia
(First published in book form in 1823)

ON SOME OF THE OLD ACTORS

BENSLEY... threw over the part [of Malvolio] an air of
Spanish loftiness. He looked, spake, and moved like an old
Castilian. He was starch, spruce, opinionated, but his
superstructure of pride seemed bottomed upon a sense of
worth. There was something in it beyond the coxcomb.
It was big and swelling, but you could not be sure that it
was hollow. You might wish to see it taken down, but you
felt that it was upon an elevation. He was magnificent from
the outset; but when the decent sobrieties of the character
began to give way, and the poison of self-love, in his conceit
of the Countess's affection, gradually to work, you would
have thought that the hero of La Mancha in person stood
before you. How he went smiling to himself! with what
ineffable carelessness would he twirl his gold chain! what
a dream it was! you were infected with the illusion, and
did not wish that it should be removed! you had no room
for laughter! if an unseasonable reflection of morality
obtruded itself, it was a deep sense of the pitiable infirmity
of man's nature, that can lay him open to such frenzies—
but in truth you rather admired than pitied the lunacy
while it lasted—you felt that an hour of such mistake was
worth an age with the eyes open. Who would not wish to

live but for a day in the conceit of such a lady's love as Olivia? Why, the Duke would have given his principality but for a quarter of a minute, sleeping or waking, to have been so deluded. The man seemed to tread upon air, to taste manna, to walk with his head in the clouds, to mate Hyperion. O! shake not the castles of his pride—endure yet for a season bright moments of confidence—'stand still ye watches of the element', that Malvolio may be still in fancy fair Olivia's lord—but fate and retribution say no—I hear the mischievous titter of Maria—the witty taunts of Sir Toby—the still more insupportable triumph of the foolish knight—the counterfeit Sir Topas is unmasked—and 'thus the whirligig of time', as the true clown hath it, 'brings in his revenges'. I confess that I never saw the catastrophe of this character, while Bensley played it, without a kind of tragic interest. There was good foolery too. Few now remember Dodd. What an Aguecheek the stage lost in him! Lovegrove, who came nearest to the old actors, revived the character some few seasons ago, and made it sufficiently grotesque; but Dodd was *it,* as it came out of Nature's hands. It might be said to remain *in puris naturalibus.* In expressing slowness of apprehension this actor surpassed all others. You could see the first dawn of an idea stealing slowly over his countenance, climbing up by little and little, with a painful process, till it cleared up at last to the fulness of a twilight conception—its highest meridian. He seemed to keep back his intellect, as some have had the power to retard their pulsation. The balloon takes less time in filling, than it took to cover the expansion of his broad moony face over all its quarters with expression. A glimmer of understanding would appear in a corner of his eye, and for lack of fuel go out again. A part of his forehead would catch a little intelligence, and be a long time in communicating it to the remainder.

THOMAS DE QUINCEY
1785–1859

Confessions of an English Opium-eater
(First edition 1822)

THE PAINS OF OPIUM

MAY 1818. . . . All this, and much more than I can say, the reader must enter into before he can comprehend the unimaginable horror which these dreams of oriental imagery and mythological tortures impressed upon me. Under the connecting feeling of tropical heat and vertical sunlights, I brought together all creatures, birds, beasts, reptiles, all trees and plants, usages and appearances, that are found in all tropical regions, and assembled them together in China or Hindostan. From kindred feelings, I soon brought Egypt and her gods under the same law. I was stared at, hooted at, grinned at, chattered at, by monkeys, by paroquets, by cockatoos. I ran into pagodas, and was fixed for centuries at the summit, or in secret rooms; I was the idol; I was the priest; I was worshipped; I was sacrificed. I fled from the wrath of Brama through all the forests of Asia; Vishnu hated me; Siva lay in wait for me. I came suddenly upon Isis and Osiris: I had done a deed, they said, which the ibis and the crocodile trembled at. Thousands of years I lived and was buried in stone coffins, with mummies and sphinxes, in narrow chambers at the heart of eternal pyramids. I was kissed, with cancerous kisses, by crocodiles, and was laid, confounded with all unutterable abortions, amongst reeds and Nilotic mud.

Some slight abstraction I thus attempt of my oriental dreams, which filled me always with such amazement at the monstrous scenery that horror seemed absorbed for a while in sheer astonishment. Sooner or later came a reflux of feeling that swallowed up the astonishment, and left me, not so much in terror, as in hatred and abomination of what I saw. Over every form, and threat, and punishment, and dim sightless incarceration, brooded a killing sense of eternity and infinity. Into these dreams only it was, with one or two slight exceptions, that any circumstances of physical horror entered. All before had been moral and spiritual terrors. But here the main agents were ugly birds, or snakes, or crocodiles, especially the last. The cursed crocodile became to me the object of more horror than all the rest. I was compelled to live with him; and (as was always the case in my dreams) for centuries. Sometimes I escaped, and found myself in Chinese houses. All the feet of the tables, sofas, etc., soon became instinct with life: the abominable head of the crocodile, and his leering eyes, looked out at me, multiplied into ten thousand repetitions; and I stood loathing and fascinated. So often did this hideous reptile haunt my dreams that many times the very same dream was broken up in the very same way: I heard gentle voices speaking to me (I hear everything when I am sleeping), and instantly I awoke; it was broad noon, and my children were standing, hand in hand, at my bedside, come to show me their coloured shoes, or new frocks, or to let me see them dressed for going out. No experience was so awful to me, and at the same time so pathetic, as this abrupt translation from the darkness of the infinite to the gaudy summer air of highest noon, and from the unutterable abortions of miscreated gigantic vermin to the sight of infancy and innocent *human* natures.

WALTER SAVAGE LANDOR
1775–1864

Imaginary Conversations
(First edition 1824–9)

SOUTHEY AND PORSON

PORSON.... But would you on the whole compare Cowper with Dryden?

SOUTHEY. Dryden possesses a much richer store of thoughts, expatiates upon more topics, has more vigour, vivacity, and animation. He is always shrewd and penetrating, explicit and perspicuous, concise where conciseness is desirable, and copious where copiousness can yield delight. When he aims at what is highest in poetry, the dramatic, he falls below his *Fables*. However, I would not compare the poetical power of Cowper with his; nor would I, as some have done, pit Young against him. Young is too often fantastical and frivolous: he pins butterflies to the pulpit-cushion; he suspends against the grating of the charnel-house coloured lamps and comic transparencies,— Cupid, and the cat and the fiddle; he opens a store-house filled with minute particles of heterogeneous wisdom and unpalatable gobbets of ill-concocted learning, contributions from the classics, from the schoolmen, from homilies, and from farces. What you expect to be an elegy turns out an epigram; and when you think he is bursting into tears, he laughs in your face. Do you go with him into his closet, prepared for an admonition or a rebuke, he shakes his head, and you sneeze at the powder and perfumery of his peruke. Wonder not if I prefer to his pungent essences the incense which Cowper burns before the altar.

PORSON.... Cowper plays in the play-ground, and not in the churchyard. Nothing of his is out of place or out of season. He possessed a rich vein of ridicule; but he turned it to good account, opening it on prig parsons, and graver and worse impostors. He was among the first who put to flight the mischievous little imps of allegory, so cherished and fondled by the Wartons. They are as bad in poetry as mice in a cheese-room. You poets are still rather too fond of the unsubstantial. Some will have nothing else than what they call pure imagination. Now air-plants ought not to fill the whole conservatory; other plants, I would modestly suggest, are worth cultivating, which send their roots pretty deep into the ground. I hate both poetry and wine without body. Look at Shakespeare, Bacon and Milton; were these your pure imagination men? The least of them whichever it was, carried a jewel of poetry about him worth all his tribe that came after. Did the two of them who wrote in verse build upon nothing? Did their predecessors? And, pray, whose daughter was the Muse they invoked? Why, Memory's. They stood among substantial men, and sang upon recorded actions. The plain of Scamander, the promontory of Sigaeum, the palaces of Tros and Dardanus, the citadel in which the Fates sang mournfully under the image of Minerva, seem fitter places for the Muses to alight on, than artificial rockwork or than fairy rings. But your great favourite, I hear, is Spenser, who shines in allegory, and who, like an aerolite is dull and heavy when he descends to the ground.

SOUTHEY. He continues a great favourite with me still, although he must always lose a little as our youth declines; Spenser's is a spacious but somewhat low chamber, hung with rich tapestry on which the figures are mostly disproportioned, but some of the faces are lively and beautiful; the furniture is part creaking and worm-eaten, part fragrant with cedar and sandal-wood and aromatic gums and balsams; every table and mantelpiece and cabinet is covered with gorgeous vases, and birds, and dragons, and houses in the air.

PORSON. There is scarcely a poet of the same eminence, whom I have found it so delightful to read in, or so tedious to read through. Give me Chaucer in preference. He slaps us on the shoulder, and makes us spring up while the dew is on the grass, and while the long shadows play about it in all quarters. We feel strong with the freshness round us, and we return with a keener appetite, having such a companion in our walk . . . .

THOMAS CARLYLE
1795–1881

The French Revolution
(First edition 1837)

PART III, BOOK II, CHAPTER VII:
PLACE DE LA RÉVOLUTION

THROUGH the rest of the streets there is silence as of the
grave. No man not armed is allowed to be there: the
armed, did any even pity, dare not express it, each man
overawed by all his neighbours. All windows are down,
none seen looking through them. All shops are shut. No
wheel-carriage rolls, this morning, in these streets but
one only.

Eighty thousand armed men stand ranked, like armed
statues of men; cannons bristle, cannoneers with match
burning, but no word or movement: it is as a city enchant-
ed into silence and stone: one carriage with its escort,
slowly rumbling, is the only sound. Louis reads in his Book
of Devotion, the Prayers of the Dying: clatter of this death-
march falls sharp on the ear, in the great silence: but the
thought would fain struggle heavenward, and forget the
Earth.

As the clocks strike ten, behold the Place de la Révolution, once Place de Louis Quinze: the Guillotine, mounted
near the old pedestal where stood the Statue of that Louis!
Far around, all bristles with cannons and armed men:
spectators crowding in the rear: D'Orléans Égalité there in
cabriolet. Swift messengers, *hoquetons,* speed to the Town

Hall, every three minutes: near by is the Convention sitting—vengeful for Lepelletier. Heedless of all, Louis reads his Prayers of the Dying; not till five minutes yet has he finished; then the Carriage opens. What temper is he in? Ten different witnesses will give ten different accounts of it. He is in the collision of all tempers; arrived now at the black Mahlstrom and descent of Death: in sorrow, in indignation, in resignation struggling to be resigned. 'Take care of M. Edgeworth' he straitly charges the Lieutenant who is sitting with them: then they two descend.

The Drums are beating: *'Taisez-vous,* Silence!' he cries 'in a terrible voice, *d'une voix terrible'.* He mounts the scaffold, not without delay; he is in puce coat, breeches of grey, white stockings. He strips off the coat; stands disclosed in a sleeve-waistcoat of white flannel. The Executioners approach to bind him: he spurns, resists; Abbé Edgeworth has to remind him how the Saviour, in whom men trust, submitted to be bound. His hands are tied, his head bare; the fatal moment is come. He advances to the edge of the Scaffold 'his face very red', and says 'Frenchmen, I die innocent: it is from the Scaffold and near appearing before God that I tell you so. I pardon my enemies; I desire that France . . .'. A General on horseback, Santerre or another, prances out, with uplifted hand: *'Tambours!'* The drums drown the voice. 'Executioners, do your duty!' The Executioners, desperate lest themselves be murdered (for Santerre and his armed Ranks will strike, if they do not) seize the hapless Louis: six of them desperate, him singly desperate, struggling there; and bind him to their plank. Abbé Edgeworth, stooping, bespeaks him: 'Son of Saint Louis, ascend to Heaven'. The Axe clanks down, a King's life is shorn away. It is Monday the 21st of January 1793. He was aged thirty-eight years four months and twenty-eight days.

THOMAS BABINGTON MACAULAY, LORD MACAULAY
1800–59

Critical and Historical Essays
(First edition 1843)

ON SIR JAMES MACKINTOSH'S HISTORY OF THE
REVOLUTION IN ENGLAND, IN 1688

CHARLES II

THEN commenced the reflux of public opinion. The nation began to find out to what a man it had entrusted, without conditions, all its dearest interests, on what a man it had lavished all its fondest affection. On the ignoble nature of the restored exile, adversity had exhausted all her discipline in vain. He had one immense advantage over most other princes. Though born in the purple, he was far better acquainted with the vicissitudes of life and the diversities of character than most of his subjects. He had known restraint, danger, penury, and dependence. He had often suffered from ingratitude, insolence, and treachery. He had received many signal proofs of faithful and heroic attachment. He had seen, if ever man saw, both sides of human nature. But only one side remained in his memory. He had learned only to despise and to distrust his species, to consider integrity in men, and modesty in women, as mere acting; nor did he think it worth while to keep his opinion to himself. He was incapable of friendship; yet he was perpetually led by favourites without being in the smallest degree duped by them. He knew their regard to his interests was all simulated; but, from a certain easiness which had no connection with humanity, he submitted, half-laughing at himself, to be made the tool of any woman whose person attracted him, or of any man whose tattle diverted him. He thought little and cared less about religion. He seems to have spent his life in dawdling suspense between Hobbism and Popery. He was crowned in his youth with the Covenant in his hand; he died at last with the Host sticking in his throat; and during most of the intermediate years, was occupied in persecuting both Covenanters and Catholics. He was not a tyrant from the ordinary motives. He valued power for its own sake little, and fame still less. He does not appear to have been vindictive, or to have found any pleasing excitement in cruelty. What he wanted was to be amused, to get through the twenty-four hours pleasantly without sitting down to dry business. Sauntering was, as Sheffield expresses it, the true Sultana Queen of His Majesty's affections. A sitting in council would have been insupportable to him if the Duke of Buckingham had not been there to make mouths at the Chancellor. It has been said, and is highly probable, that in his exile he was quite disposed to sell his rights to Cromwell for a good round sum. To the last, his only quarrel with his Parliaments was that they often gave him trouble and would not always give him money. If there was a person for whom he felt a real regard that person was his brother. If there was a point about which he really entertained a scruple of conscience or of honour, that point was the descent of the crown. Yet he was willing to consent to the Exclusion Bill for six hundred thousand pounds; and the negotiation was broken off only because he insisted on being paid beforehand. To do him justice, his temper was good; his manners agreeable; his natural talents above mediocrity. But he was sensual, frivolous, false, and cold-hearted, beyond almost any prince of whom history makes mention.

EMILY BRONTË
1818–48

Wuthering Heights
(First edition 1847)

CHAPTER IX

ERE this speech ended, I became sensible of Heathcliff's presence. Having noticed a slight movement, I turned my head, and saw him rise from the bench, and steal out noiselessly. He had listened till he heard Catherine say it would degrade her to marry him, and then he stayed to hear no further. My companion, sitting on the ground, was prevented by the back of the settle from remarking his presence or departure; but I started, and bade her hush!

'Why?' she asked, gazing nervously round.

'Joseph is here,' I answered, catching opportunely the roll of his cart-wheels up the road; 'and Heathcliff will come in with him. I'm not sure whether he were not at the door this moment.'

'Oh, he couldn't overhear me at the door!' said she. 'Give me Hareton, while you get the supper, and when it is ready ask me to sup with you. I want to cheat my uncomfortable conscience, and be convinced that Heathcliff has no notion of these things. He has not, has he? He does not know what being in love is?'

'I see no reason that he should not know, as well as you,' I returned; 'and if you are his choice, he'll be the most unfortunate creature that ever was born! As soon as you become Mrs. Linton, he loses friend, and love, and all! Have you considered how you'll bear the separation, and how he'll bear to be quite deserted in the world? Because, Miss Catherine—'

'He quite deserted! we separated!' she exclaimed, with an accent of indignation. 'Who is to separate us, pray? They'll meet the fate of Milo! Not as long as I live, Ellen: for no mortal creature. Every Linton on the face of the earth might melt into nothing, before I could consent to forsake Heathcliff. Oh, that's not what I intend—that's not what I mean! I shouldn't be Mrs Linton were such a price demanded! He'll be as much to me as he has been all his lifetime. Edgar must shake off his antipathy, and tolerate him at least. He will, when he learns my true feelings towards him. Nelly, I see now, you think me a selfish wretch; but did it never strike you that if Heathcliff and I married, we should be beggars? whereas, if I marry Linton,

I can aid Heathcliff to rise, and place him out of my
brother's power.'

'With your husband's money, Miss Catherine?' I asked.
'You'll find him not so pliable as you calculate upon: and,
though I'm hardly a judge, I think that's the worst motive
you've given yet for being the wife of young Linton.'

'It is not,' retorted she; 'it is the best! The others were the
satisfaction of my whims: and for Edgar's sake, too, to
satisfy him. This is for the sake of one who comprehends
in his person my feelings to Edgar and myself. I cannot
express it; but surely you and everybody have a notion that
there is or should be an existence of yours beyond you.
What were the use of my creation, if I were entirely contained here? My great miseries in this world have been
Heathcliff's miseries, and I watched and felt each from the
beginning: my great thought in living is himself. If all else
perished, and *he* remained, *I* should still continue to be;
and if all else remained, and he were annihilated, the
universe would turn to a mighty stranger: I should not
seem a part of it. My love for Linton is like the foliage in
the woods: time will change it, I'm well aware, as winter
changes the trees. My love for Heathcliff resembles the
eternal rocks beneath: a source of little visible delight, but
necessary. Nelly, I *am* Heathcliff! He's always, always in my
mind: not as a pleasure, any more than I am always a
pleasure to myself, but as my own being . . . .'

CHARLOTTE BRONTË
1816–55

Villette
(First edition 1853)

CHAPTER XXIX: MONSIEUR'S FÊTE

In the course of the afternoon . . . I descended to the
schoolroom. It slept in holiday repose. The day-pupils were
all gone home, the boarders were out walking, the teachers,
except the surveillante of the week, were in town, visiting
or shopping; the suite of divisions was vacant; so was the
grand salle, with its huge solemn globe hanging in the
midst, its pair of many-branched chandeliers, and its
horizontal grand piano, closed, silent, enjoying its mid-
week Sabbath. I rather wondered to find the first classe
door ajar; this room being usually locked when empty,
and being then inaccessible to any save Madame Beck and
myself, who possessed a duplicate key. I wondered still
more, on approaching, to hear a vague movement as of life
—a step, a chair stirred, a sound like the opening of a desk.

'It is only Madame Beck doing inspection duty', was the
conclusion following a moment's reflection. The partially
opened door gave opportunity for assurance on this point.
I looked. Behold! not the inspecting garb of Madame
Beck—the shawl and the clean cap—but the coat, and the
close-shorn dark head of a man. This person occupied my
chair; his olive hand held my desk open, his nose was lost
to view amongst my papers. His back was towards me, but
there could be not a moment's question about identity.

Already was the attire of ceremony discarded: the cherished and ink-stained paletôt was resumed; the perverse bonnet-grec lay on the floor, as if just dropped from the hand, culpably busy.

Now I knew, and I had long known, that that hand of M. Emanuel's was on the most intimate terms with my desk; that it raised and lowered the lid, ransacked and arranged the contents, almost as familiarly as my own. The fact was not dubious, nor did he wish it to be so: he left signs of each visit palpable and unmistakable; hitherto, however, I had never caught him in the act: watch as I would, I could not detect the hours and moments of his coming. I saw the brownies' work in exercises left overnight full of faults, and found next morning carefully corrected: I profited by his capricious good-will in loans full welcome and refreshing. Between a sallow dictionary and worn-out grammar would magically grow a fresh interesting new work, or a classic, mellow and sweet in its ripe age. Out of my work-basket would laughingly peep a romance, under it would lurk the pamphlet, the magazine, whence last evening's reading had been extracted. Impossible to doubt the source whence these treasures flowed: had there been no other indication, one condemning and traitor peculiarity common to them all, settled the question—*they smelt of cigars.* This was very shocking, of course: *I* thought so at first, and used to open the window with some bustle, to air my desk, and with fastidious finger and thumb to hold the peccant brochures forth to the purifying breeze. I was cured of that formality suddenly. Monsieur caught me at it one day, understood the inference, instantly relieved my hand of its burden, and, in another moment, would have thrust the same into the glowing stove. It chanced to be a book, on the perusal of which I was bent; so for once I proved as decided and quicker than himself; recaptured the spoil, and—having saved this volume—never hazarded a second. With all this, I had never yet been able to arrest in his visits the freakish, friendly, cigar-loving phantom.

But now at last I had him: there he was—the very brownie himself; and there, curling from his lips, was the pale blue breath of his Indian darling: he was smoking into my desk: it might well betray him. Provoked at this particular, and yet pleased to surprise him—pleased, that is, with the mixed feeling of the housewife who discovers at last her strange elfin ally busy in the dairy at the untimely churn—I softly stole forward, stood behind him, bent with precaution over his shoulder.

My heart smote me to see that—after this morning's hostility, after my seeming remissness, after the puncture experienced by his feelings, and the ruffling undergone by his temper—he, all-willing to forget and forgive, had brought me a couple of handsome volumes, of which the title and authorship were guarantees for interest. Now, as he sat bending above the desk, he was stirring up its contents; but with gentle and careful hand; disarranging indeed, but not harming. My heart smote me: as I bent over him, as he sat unconscious, doing me what good he could, and I daresay not feeling towards me unkindly, my morning's anger quite melted: I did not dislike Professor Emanuel.

CHARLES DICKENS
1812–70

The Posthumous Papers of the Pickwick Club
(First edition 1836–7)

CHAPTER XXXIV IS WHOLLY DEVOTED TO A FULL AND
FAITHFUL REPORT OF THE MEMORABLE TRIAL OF
BARDELL AGAINST PICKWICK

IT was quite unnecessary to call Samuel Weller; for Samuel
Weller stepped briskly into the box the instant his name
was pronounced; and placing his hat on the floor, and his
arms on the rail, took a bird's eye view of the bar, and a
comprehensive survey of the bench, with a remarkably
cheerful and lively aspect.

'What's your name, sir?' inquired the judge.

'Sam Weller, my lord,' replied that gentleman.

'Do you spell it with a "V" or a "W"?' inquired the judge.

'That depends upon the taste and fancy of the speller,
my lord,' replied Sam; 'I never had occasion to spell it more
than once or twice in my life, but I spells it with a "V".'

Here a voice in the gallery exclaimed aloud, 'Quite right
too, Samivel, quite right. Put it down a we, my lord, put
it down a we.'

'Who is that, who dares to address the court?' asked the
little judge, looking up. 'Usher.'

'Yes, my lord.'

'Bring that person here instantly.'

'Yes, my lord.'

But as the usher didn't find the person, he didn't bring him; and after a great commotion, all the people who had got up to look for the culprit, sat down again. The little judge turned to the witness as soon as his indignation would allow him to speak, and said,

'Do you know who that was, sir?'

'I rayther suspect it was my father, my lord,' replied Sam.

'Do you see him here now?' said the judge.

'No, I don't, my lord,' replied Sam, staring right up into the lantern in the roof of the court.

'If you could have pointed him out, I would have committed him instantly,' said the judge.

Sam bowed his acknowledgments and turned, with unimpaired cheerfulness of countenance, towards Serjeant Buzfuz.

'Now, Mr Weller,' said Serjeant Buzfuz.

'Now, sir,' replied Sam.

'I believe you are in the service of Mr Pickwick, the defendant in this case. Speak up, if you please, Mr Weller.'

'I mean to speak up, sir,' replied Sam; 'I am in the service o' that 'ere gen'l'man, and a wery good service it is.'

'Little to do, and plenty to get, I suppose?' said Serjeant Buzfuz, with jocularity.

'Oh, quite enough to get, sir, as the soldier said ven they ordered him three hundred and fifty lashes,' replied Sam.

'You must not tell us what the soldier, or any other man, said, sir,' interposed the judge; 'it's not evidence.'

'Wery good, my lord,' replied Sam.

'Do you recollect anything particular happening on the morning when you were first engaged by the defendant; eh, Mr Weller?' said Serjeant Buzfuz.

'Yes I do, sir,' replied Sam.

'Have the goodness to tell the jury what it was.'

'I had a reg'lar new fit out o' clothes that mornin', gen'l'men of the jury,' said Sam, 'and that was a wery partickler and uncommon circumstance vith me in those days.'

Hereupon there was a general laugh; and the little judge, looking with an angry countenance over his desk, said, 'You had better be careful, sir.'

'So Mr Pickwick said at the time my lord,' replied Sam; 'and I was wery careful o' that 'ere suit of clothes; wery careful indeed, my lord.'

The judge looked sternly at Sam for full two minutes, but Sam's features were so perfectly calm and serene that the judge said nothing, and motioned Serjeant Buzfuz to proceed.

'Do you mean to tell me, Mr Weller,' said Serjeant Buzfuz, folding his arms emphatically, and turning half-round to the jury, as if in mute assurance that he would bother the witness yet: 'Do you mean to tell me, Mr Weller, that you saw nothing of this fainting on the part of the plaintiff in the arms of the defendant, which you have heard described by the witnesses?'

'Certainly not,' replied Sam. 'I was in the passage 'till they called me up, and then the old lady was not there.'

'Now, attend, Mr Weller,' said Serjeant Buzfuz, dipping

a large pen into the inkstand before him, for the purpose of frightening Sam with a show of taking down his answer. 'You were in the passage, and yet saw nothing of what was going forward. Have you a pair of eyes, Mr Weller?'

'Yes, I have a pair of eyes,' replied Sam, 'and that's just it. If they wos a pair o' patent double million magnifyin' gas microscopes of hextra power, p'raps I might be able to see through a flight of stairs, and a deal door; but bein' only eyes, you see, my wision's limited.'

At this answer, which was delivered without the slightest appearance of irritation, and with the most complete simplicity and equanimity of manner, the spectators tittered, the little judge smiled, and Serjeant Buzfuz looked particularly foolish.

WILLIAM MAKEPEACE THACKERAY
1811–63

Vanity Fair
(First edition 1847–8)

CHAPTER LXV: FULL OF BUSINESS AND PLEASURE

THE gentleman from Bengal was standing disconcerted by this incident, when the door of no. 92 opened of itself, and Becky's little head peeped out full of archness and mischief. She lighted on Jos. 'It's you,' she said, coming out. 'How I have been waiting for you! Stop, not yet—in one minute you shall come in.' In that instant she put a rouge-pot, a brandy-bottle, and a plate of broken meat into the bed, gave one smooth to her hair, and finally let in her visitor.

She had, by way of morning robe, a pink domino, a trifle faded and soiled, and marked here and there with pomatum; but her arms shone out from the loose sleeves of the dress very white and fair, and it was tied round her little waist, so as not ill to set off the trim little figure of the wearer. She led Jos by the hand into her garret. 'Come in,' she said. 'Come, and talk to me. Sit yonder on the chair'; and she gave the Civilian's hand a little squeeze, and laughingly placed him upon it. As for herself, she placed herself on the bed—not on the bottle and plate, you may be sure—on which Jos might have reposed, had he chosen that seat; and so there she sate and talked with her old admirer.

'How little years have changed you,' she said, with a look of tender interest. 'I should have known you anywhere. What a comfort it is amongst strangers to see once more the frank honest face of an old friend!'

The frank honest face, to tell the truth, at this moment bore any expression but one of openness and honesty: it was, on the contrary, much perturbed and puzzled in look. Jos was surveying the queer little apartment in which he found his old flame. One of her gowns hung over the bed, another depending from a hook of the door: her bonnet obscured half the looking-glass, on which, too, lay the prettiest little pair of bronze boots; a French novel was on the table by the bedside, with a candle not of wax. Becky thought of popping that into the bed too, but she only put in the little paper nightcap with which she had put the candle out on going to sleep.—'I should have known you anywhere,' she continued; 'a woman never forgets some things. And you were the first man I ever—I ever saw.'

'Was I, really?' said Jos. 'God bless my soul, you—you don't say so.'

'When I came with your sister from Chiswick, I was scarcely more than a child,' Becky said. 'How is that dear love? Oh, her husband was a sad wicked man, and of course it was of me that the poor dear was jealous. As if I cared about him, heigho! when there was somebody—but no—don't let us talk of old times'; and she passed her handkerchief with the tattered lace across her eyelids.

'Is not this a strange place,' she continued, 'for a woman, who has lived in a very different world too, to be found in? I have had so many griefs and wrongs, Joseph Sedley, I have been made to suffer so cruelly, that I am almost made mad sometimes. I can't stay still in any place, but wander about always restless and unhappy. All my friends have been false to me—all. There is no such thing as an honest man in the world. I was the truest wife that ever lived, though I married my husband out of pique, because somebody else—but never mind that. I was true, and he trampled upon me, and deserted me. I was the fondest mother. I had but one child, one darling, one hope, one joy, which I held to my heart with a mother's affection, which was my life, my prayer, my—my blessing; and they—they tore it from me—tore it from me'; and she put her hand to her heart with a passionate gesture of despair, burying her face for a moment on the bed.

The brandy-bottle inside clinked up against the plate

which held the cold sausage. Both were moved, no doubt, by the exhibition of so much grief. Max and Fritz were at the door listening with wonder to Mrs Becky's sobs and cries. Jos, too, was a good deal frightened and affected at seeing his old flame in this condition. And she began, forthwith, to tell her story—a tale so neat, simple, and artless, that it was quite evident from hearing her, that if ever there was a white-robed angel escaped from heaven to be subject to the infernal machinations and villainy of fiends here below, that spotless being—that miserable un-sullied martyr, was present on the bed before Jos—on the bed, sitting on the brandy-bottle.

JOHN RUSKIN
1819–1900

Modern Painters
(First edition 1843–60)

(VOL. I, SECTION V: OF TRUTH OF WATER)
CHAPTER III: OF WATER AS PAINTED BY TURNER

BUT, I think, the noblest sea that Turner has ever painted, and, if so, the noblest certainly ever painted by man, is that of the Slave Ship, the chief Academy picture of the Exhibition of 1840. It is a sunset on the Atlantic, after prolonged storm; but the storm is partially lulled, and the torn and streaming rain-clouds are moving in scarlet lines to lose themselves in the hollow of the night. The whole surface of sea included in the picture is divided into two ridges of enormous swell, not high, nor local, but a low, broad heaving of the whole ocean, like the lifting of its bosom by deep-drawn breath after the torture of the storm. Between these two ridges the fire of the sunset falls along the trough of the sea, dyeing it with an awful but glorious light, the intense and lurid splendour which burns like gold, and bathes like blood. Along this fiery path and valley, the tossing waves by which the swell of the sea is restlessly divided, lift themselves in dark, indefinite, fantastic forms, each casting a faint and ghastly shadow behind it along the illumined foam. They do not rise everywhere, but three or four together in wild groups, fitfully and furiously, as the under strength of the swell compels or permits them; leaving between them treacherous spaces of level and whirling water, now lighted with green and lamp-like fire, now flashing back the gold of the declining sun, now fearfully dyed from above with the indistinguishable images of the burning clouds, which fall upon them in flakes of crimson and scarlet, and give to the reckless waves the added motion of their own fiery flying. Purple and blue, the lurid shadows of the hollow breakers are cast upon the mist of the night, which gathers cold and low, advancing like the shadow of death upon the guilty ship as it labours amidst the lightning of the sea, its thin masts written upon the sky in lines of blood, girded with condemnation in that fearful hue which signs the sky with horror, and mixes its flaming flood with the sunlight—and cast far along the desolate heave of the sepulchral waves, incarnadines the multitudinous sea.

I believe, if I were reduced to rest Turner's immortality

upon any single work, I should choose this. Its daring conception—ideal in the highest sense of the word—is based on the purest truth, and wrought out with the concentrated knowledge of a life; its colour is absolutely perfect, not one false or morbid hue in any part or line, and so modulated that every square inch of canvas is a perfect composition; its drawing as accurate as fearless; the ship buoyant, bending, and full of motion; its tones as true as they are wonderful; and the whole picture dedicated to the most sublime of subjects and impressions—(completing thus the perfect system of all truth, which we have shown to be formed by Turner's works)—the power, majesty, and deathfulness of the open, deep, illimitable sea.

WALTER PATER

1839–94

The Renaissance

(First edition 1873)

SANDRO BOTTICELLI

WHAT is strangest is that [Botticelli] carries this sentiment into classical subjects, its most complete expression being a picture in the *Uffizi,* of Venus rising from the sea, in which the grotesque emblems of the middle age, and a landscape full of its peculiar feeling, and even its strange draperies, powdered all over in the Gothic manner with a quaint conceit of daisies, frame a figure that reminds you of the faultless nude studies of Ingres. At first, perhaps, you are attracted only by a quaintness of design, which seems to recall all at once whatever you have read of Florence in the fifteenth century; afterwards you may think that this quaintness must be incongruous with the subject, and that the colour is cadaverous or at least cold. And yet, the more you come to understand what imaginative colouring really is, that all colour is no mere delightful quality of natural things, but a spirit upon them by which they become expressive to the spirit, the better you will like this peculiar quality of colour; and you will find that quaint design of Botticelli's a more direct inlet into the Greek temper than the works of the Greeks themselves even of the finest period. Of the Greeks as they really were, of their difference from ourselves, of the aspects of their outward life, we know far more than Botticelli, or his most learned contemporaries; but for us, long familiarity has taken off the edge of the lesson, and we are hardly conscious of what we owe to the Hellenic spirit. But in pictures like this of Botticelli's you have a record of the first impression made by it on minds turned back towards it, in almost painful aspiration, from a world in which it had been ignored so long; and in the passion, the energy, the industry of real-isation, with which Botticelli carries out his intention, is the exact measure of the legitimate influence over the human mind of the imaginative system of which this is the central myth. The light is indeed cold—mere sunless dawn; but a later painter would have cloyed you with sunshine; and you can see the better for that quietness in the morning air each long promontory as it slopes down to the water's edge. Men go forth to their labours until the evening; but she is awake before them, and you might think that the sorrow in her face was at the thought of the whole long day of love yet to come. An emblematical figure of the wind blows hard across the grey water, moving forward the dainty-lipped shell on which she sails, the sea 'showing his teeth' as it moves in thin lines of foam, and sucking in, one by one, the falling roses, each severe in outline, plucked off short at the stalk, but embrowned a little, as Botticelli's flowers always are. Botticelli meant all that imagery to be altogether pleasurable; and it was partly an incompleteness of resources, inseparable from the art of that time, that subdued and chilled it; but his predilection for minor tones counts also; and what is unmistakeable is the sadness with which he has conceived the goddess of pleasure, as the depositary of a great power over the lives of men.

JOHN HENRY NEWMAN
1801–90

Apologia Pro Vita Sua
(First edition 1864)

PART IV. HISTORY OF MY RELIGIOUS OPINIONS, 1833–9

I SAW indeed clearly that my place in the Movement was lost; public confidence was at an end; my occupation was gone. It was simply an impossibility that I could say any thing henceforth to good effect, when I had been posted up by the marshal on the buttery-hatch of every College of my University, after the manner of discommoned pastry-cooks, and when in every part of the country and every class of society, through every organ and opportunity of opinion, in newspapers, in periodicals, at meetings, in pulpits, at dinner-tables, in coffee-rooms, in railway carriages, I was denounced as a traitor who had laid his train and was detected in the very act of firing it against the time-honoured Establishment. There were indeed men, besides my own immediate friends, men of name and position, who gallantly took my part, as Dr Hook, Mr Palmer, and Mr Perceval; it must have been a grievous trial for themselves; yet what after all could they do for me? Confidence in me was lost;—but I had already lost full confidence in myself. Thoughts had passed over me a year and a half before in respect to the Anglican claims, which for the time had profoundly troubled me. They had gone: I had not less confidence in the power and the prospects of the Apostolical movement than before; not less confidence than before in the grievousness of what I called the 'dominant errors' of Rome; but how was I any more to have absolute confidence in myself? how was I to have confidence in my present confidence? how was I to be sure that I should always think as I thought now? I felt that by this event a kind Providence had saved me from an impossible position in the future.

First, if I remember right, they wished me to withdraw the Tract. This I refused to do: I would not do so for the sake of those who were unsettled or in danger of unsettlement. I would not do so for my own sake; for how could I acquiesce in a mere Protestant interpretation of the

Articles? how could I range myself among the professors of a theology, of which it put my teeth on edge even to hear the sound?

Next they said, 'Keep silence; do not defend the Tract'; I answered, 'Yes, if you will not condemn it,—if you will allow it to continue on sale'. They pressed on me whenever I gave way; they fell back when they saw me obstinate. Their line of action was to get out of me as much as they could; but upon the point of their tolerating the Tract I *was* obstinate. So they let me continue it on sale; and they said they would not condemn it. But they said that this was on condition that I did not defend it, that I stopped the series, and that I myself published my own condemnation in a letter to the Bishop of Oxford. I impute nothing whatever to him, he was ever most kind to me. Also, they said they could not answer for what some individual Bishops might perhaps say about the Tract in their own charges. I agreed to their conditions. My one point was to save the Tract.

Not a line in writing was given me, as a pledge of the observance of the main article on their side of the engagement. Parts of letters from them were read to me, without being put into my hands. It was an 'understanding'. A clever man had warned me against 'understandings' some thirteen years before: I have hated them ever since.

MATTHEW ARNOLD

1822–88

Essays in Criticism

(First edition 1865)

PREFACE

HOWEVER, it is not merely out of modesty that I prefer to stand alone, and to concentrate on myself, as a plain citizen of the republic of letters, and not as an office-bearer in a hierarchy, the whole responsibility for all I write; it is much more out of genuine devotion to the University of Oxford, for which I feel, and always must feel, the fondest, the most reverential attachment. In an epoch of dissolution and transformation, such as that on which we are now entered, habits, ties, and associations are inevitably broken up, the action of individuals becomes more distinct, the short-comings, errors, heats, disputes, which necessarily attend individual action, are brought into greater prominence. Who would not gladly keep clear, from all these passing clouds, an august institution which was there before they arose, and which will be there when they have blown over? . . .

No, we are all seekers still! seekers often make mistakes, and I wish mine to redound to my own discredit only, and not to touch Oxford. Beautiful city! so venerable, so lovely, so unravaged by the fierce intellectual life of our century, so serene!

'There are our young barbarians, all at play!'

And yet, steeped in sentiment as she lies, spreading her gardens to the moonlight, and whispering from her towers the last enchantments of the Middle Age, who will deny that Oxford, by her ineffable charm, keeps ever calling us nearer to the true goal of all of us, to the ideal, to perfection,—to beauty, in a word, which is only truth seen from another side?—nearer, perhaps, than all the science of Tübingen. Adorable dreamer, whose heart has been so romantic! who hast given thyself so prodigally, given thyself to sides and to heroes not mine, only never to the Philistines! home of lost causes, and forsaken beliefs, and unpopular names, and impossible loyalties! what example could ever so inspire us to keep down the Philistine in ourselves, what teacher could ever so save us from that bondage to which we are all prone, that bondage which Goethe, in his incomparable lines on the death of Schiller, makes it his friend's highest praise (and nobly did Schiller deserve the praise) to have left miles out of sight behind him;—the bondage of *was uns alle bändigt,* DAS GEMEINE!' She will forgive me, even if I have unwittingly drawn upon her a shot or two aimed at her unworthy son; for she is generous, and the cause in which I fight is, after all, hers. Apparitions of a day, what is our puny warfare against the Philistines, compared with the warfare which this queen of romance has been waging against them for centuries, and will wage after we are gone?

GEORGE ELIOT
1819–80
The Mill on the Floss
(First edition 1860)

BOOK I, CHAPTER IX: TO GARUM FIRS

... THEY went in procession along the bright and slippery corridor, dimly lighted by the semi-lunar top of the window which rose above the closed shutter: it was really quite solemn. Aunt Pullet paused and unlocked a door which opened on something still more solemn than the passage: a darkened room, in which the outer light, entering feebly, showed what looked like the corpses of furniture in white shrouds. Everything that was not shrouded stood with its legs upwards. Lucy laid hold of Maggie's frock, and Maggie's heart beat rapidly.

Aunt Pullet half-opened the shutter and then unlocked the wardrobe, with a melancholy deliberateness which was quite in keeping with the funereal solemnity of the scene. The delicious scent of rose-leaves that issued from the wardrobe, made the process of taking out sheet after sheet of silver paper quite pleasant to assist at, though the sight of the bonnet at last was an anticlimax to Maggie, who would have preferred something more strikingly preternatural. But few things could have been more impressive to Mrs Tulliver. She looked all round it in silence for some moments, and then said emphatically, 'Well, sister, I'll never speak against the full crowns again!'

It was a great concession, and Mrs Pullet felt it: she felt something was due to it.

'You'd like to see it on, sister?' she said, sadly. 'I'll open the shutter a bit further.'

'Well, if you don't mind taking off your cap, sister,' said Mrs Tulliver.

Mrs Pullet took off her cap, displaying the brown silk scalp with a jutting promontory of curls which was common to the more mature and judicious women of those times, and placing the bonnet on her head, turned slowly round, like a draper's lay figure, that Mrs Tulliver might miss no point of view.

'I've sometimes thought there's a loop too much o' ribbon on this left side, sister; what do you think?' said Mrs Pullet.

Mrs Tulliver looked earnestly at the point indicated, and turned her head on one side. 'Well, I think it's best as it is; if you meddled with it, sister, you might repent.'

'That's true,' said Aunt Pullet, taking off the bonnet and looking at it contemplatively.

'How much might she charge you for that bonnet, sister?' said Mrs Tulliver, whose mind was actively engaged on the possibility of getting a humble imitation of this chef-d'œuvre made from a piece of silk she had at home.

Mrs Pullet screwed up her mouth and shook her head, and then whispered, 'Pullet pays for it; he said I was to have the best bonnet at Garum Church, let the next best be whose it would'.

She began slowly to adjust the trimmings, in preparation for returning it to its place in the wardrobe, and her thoughts seemed to have taken a melancholy turn, for she shook her head.

'Ah,' she said at last, 'I may never wear it twice, sister, who knows?'

'Don't talk o' that, sister,' answered Mrs Tulliver. 'I hope you'll have your health this summer.'

'Ah! but there may come a death in the family, as there did soon after I had my green satin bonnet. Cousin Abbott may go, and we can't think o' wearing crape less nor half a year for him.'

'That would be unlucky,' said Mrs Tulliver, entering thoroughly into the possibility of an inopportune decease. 'There's never so much pleasure i' wearing a bonnet the second year, especially when the crowns are so chancy—never two summers alike.'

'Ah, it's the way i' this world,' said Mrs Pullet, returning the bonnet to the wardrobe and locking it up. She maintained a silence characterised by head-shaking, until they had all issued from the solemn chamber and were in her own room again. Then, beginning to cry, she said, 'Sister, if you should never see that bonnet again till I'm dead and gone, you'll remember I showed it you this day'.

THOMAS HARDY
1840–1928

Tess of the d'Urbervilles
(First edition 1891)

PHASE THE FOURTH, CHAPTER XXVII

NOT a human being was out of doors at the dairy. The denizens were all enjoying the usual afternoon nap of an hour or so which the exceedingly early hours kept in summer-time rendered a necessity. At the door the wood-hooped pails, sodden and bleached by infinite scrubbings, hung like hats on a stand upon the forked and peeled limb of an oak fixed there for that purpose; all of them ready and dry for the evening milking. Angel entered, and went through the silent passages of the house to the back quarters, where he listened for a moment. Sustained snores came from the cart-house, where some of the men were lying down; the grunt and squeal of sweltering pigs arose from the still further distance. The large-leaved rhubarb and cabbage plants slept too, their broad limp surfaces hanging in the sun like half-closed umbrellas.

He unbridled and fed his horse, and as he re-entered the house the clock struck three. Three was the afternoon skimming-hour; and with the stroke, Clare heard the creaking of the floor-boards above, and then the touch of a descending foot on the stairs. It was Tess's, who in another moment came down before his eyes.

She had not heard him enter, and hardly realized his presence there. She was yawning, and he saw the red interior of her mouth as if it had been a snake's. She stretched one arm so high above her coiled-up cable of hair that he could see its satin delicacy above the sunburn; her face was flushed with sleep, and her eyelids hung heavy over their pupils. The brim-fulness of her nature breathed from her. It was a moment when a woman's soul is more incarnate than at any other time; when the most spiritual beauty bespeaks itself flesh; and sex takes the outside place in the presentation.

Then those eyes flashed brightly through their filmy heaviness, before the remainder of her face was well awake. With an oddly compounded look of gladness, shyness, and surprise, she exclaimed—

'O, Mr Clare! How you frightened me—I—'

There had not at first been time for her to think of the changed relations which his declaration had introduced; but the full sense of the matter rose up in her face when she encountered Clare's tender look as he stepped forward to the bottom stair.

'Dear, darling Tessy!' he whispered, putting his arm round her, and his face to her flushed cheek. 'Don't, for Heaven's sake, Mister me any more. I have hastened back so soon because of you!'

Tess's excitable heart beat against his by way of reply; and there they stood upon the red-brick floor of the entry, the sun slanting in by the window upon his back, as he held her tightly to his breast; upon her inclining face, upon the blue veins of her temple, upon her naked arm, and her neck, and into the depths of her hair. Having been lying down in her clothes she was warm as a sunned cat. At first she would not look straight up at him, but her eyes soon lifted, and his plumbed the deepness of the ever-varying pupils, with their radiating fibrils of blue, and black, and gray, and violet, while she regarded him as Eve at her second waking might have regarded Adam.

LEWIS CARROLL
1832–98

Through the Looking-glass
(First edition 1872)

CHAPTER IX: QUEEN ALICE

... THE Red Queen drew herself up rather stiffly, and said 'Queens never make bargains.'

'I wish Queens never asked questions,' Alice thought to herself.

'Don't let us quarrel,' the White Queen said in an anxious tone. 'What is the cause of lightning?'

'The cause of lightning,' Alice said very decidedly, for she felt quite certain about this, 'is the thunder—no, no!' she hastily corrected herself. 'I meant the other way.'

'It's too late to correct it,' said the Red Queen: 'when you've once said a thing, that fixes it, and you must take the consequences.'

'Which reminds me—' the White Queen said, looking down and nervously clasping and unclasping her hands, 'we had *such* a thunderstorm last Tuesday—I mean one of the last set of Tuesdays, you know.'

Alice was puzzled. 'In *our* country,' she remarked, 'there's only one day at a time.'

The Red Queen said 'That's a poor thin way of doing things. Now *here,* we mostly have days and nights two or three at a time, and sometimes in the winter we take as many as five nights together—for warmth, you know.'

'Are five nights warmer than one night, then?' Alice ventured to ask.

'Five times as warm, of course.'

'But they should be five times as *cold,* by the same rule—'

'Just so!' cried the Red Queen. 'Five times as warm, *and* five times as cold—just as I'm five times as rich as you are, *and* five times as clever!'

Alice sighed and gave it up. 'It's exactly like a riddle with no answer!' she thought.

'Humpty Dumpty saw it too,' the White Queen went on in a low voice, more as if she were talking to herself. 'He came to the door with a corkscrew in his hand—'

'What did he want?' said the Red Queen.

'He said he *would* come in,' the White Queen went on, 'because he was looking for a hippopotamus. Now, as it happened, there wasn't such a thing in the house, that morning.'

'Is there generally?' Alice asked in an astonished tone.

'Well, only on Thursdays,' said the Queen.

'I know what he came for,' said Alice: 'he wanted to punish the fish, because—'

Here the White Queen began again. 'It was *such* a thunderstorm, you can't think!' ('She *never* could you know,' said the Red Queen.) 'And part of the roof came off, and ever so much thunder got in—and it went rolling round the room in great lumps—and knocking over the tables and things—till I was so frightened, I couldn't remember my own name!'

Alice thought to herself, 'I never should *try* to remember my name in the middle of an accident! Where would be the use of it?' but she did not say this aloud, for fear of hurting the poor Queen's feelings.

'Your Majesty must excuse her,' the Red Queen said to Alice, taking one of the White Queen's hands in her own, and gently stroking it: 'she means well, but she can't help saying foolish things, as a general rule.'

The White Queen looked timidly at Alice; she felt she *ought* to say something kind, but really couldn't think of anything at the moment.

'She never was really well brought up,' the Red Queen went on: 'But it's amazing how good-tempered she is! Pat her on the head, and see how pleased she'll be!' But this was more than Alice had courage to do.

'A little kindness—and putting her hair in papers—would do wonders with her—'

The White Queen gave a deep sigh and laid her head on Alice's shoulder. 'I *am* so sleepy' she moaned.

'She's tired, poor thing!' said the Red Queen. 'Smooth her hair—lend her your nightcap—and sing her a soothing lullaby.'

'I haven't got a nightcap with me,' said Alice, as she tried to obey the first direction: 'and I don't know any soothing lullabies.'

'I must do it myself, then,' said the Red Queen, and she began:

> Hush-a-by lady, in Alice's lap!
> Till the feast's ready, we've time for a nap:
> When the feast's over, we'll go to the ball—
> Red Queen, and White Queen, and Alice, and all!

'And now you know the words,' she added, as she put her head down on Alice's other shoulder, 'just sing it through to *me*. I'm getting sleepy, too.' In another moment both Queens were fast asleep, and snoring loud.

ROBERT LOUIS STEVENSON
1850–94

Treasure Island
(*First edition 1881–3*)

CHAPTER III: THE BLACK SPOT

... THE day after the funeral, and about three o'clock of a bitter foggy, frosty afternoon, I was standing at the door for a moment full of sad thoughts about my father, when I saw someone drawing slowly near along the road. He was plainly blind, for he tapped before him with a stick, and wore a great green shade over his eyes and nose; and he was hunched, as if with age or weakness, and wore a huge old tattered seacloak with a hood, that made him appear positively deformed. I never saw in my life a more dreadful looking figure. He stopped a little from the inn, and, raising his voice in an odd sing-song, addressed the air in front of him:

'Will any kind friend inform a poor blind man, who has lost the precious sight of his eyes in the gracious defence of his native country, England, and God bless King George! —where or in what part of this country he may now be?'

'You are at the "Admiral Benbow", Black Hill Cove, my good man,' said I.

'I hear a voice,' said he—'a young voice. Will you give me your hand, my kind young friend, and lead me in?'

I held out my hand, and the horrible, soft-spoken, eyeless creature gripped it in a moment like a vice. I was so much startled that I struggled to withdraw; but the blind man pulled me close up to him with a single action of his arm.

'Now, boy,' he said, 'take me in to the captain.'

'Sir,' said I, 'upon my word I dare not.'

'Oh,' he sneered, 'that's it! Take me in straight, or I'll break your arm.'

And he gave it, as he spoke, a wrench that made me cry out.

'Sir,' I said, 'it is for yourself I mean. The captain is not what he used to be. He sits with a drawn cutlass. Another gentleman—'

'Come now, march,' interrupted he; and I never heard a voice so cruel, and cold and ugly as that blind man's. It cowed me more than the pain; and I began to obey him at once, walking straight in at the door and towards the parlour, where our sick old buccaneer was sitting dazed with rum. The blind man clung close to me, holding me in one iron fist, and leaning almost more of his weight on me than I could carry. 'Lead me straight up to him, and when I'm in view, cry out, "Here's a friend for you, Bill". If you don't I'll do this'; and with that he gave me a twitch that I thought would have made me faint. Between this and that, I was so utterly terrified of the blind beggar that I forgot my terror of the captain, and as I opened the parlour door, cried out the words he had ordered in a trembling voice.

The poor captain raised his eyes, and at one look the rum went out of him, and left him staring sober. The expression of his face was not so much of terror as of mortal sickness. He made a movement to rise, but I do not believe he had enough force left in his body.

'Now, Bill, sit where you are,' said the beggar. 'If I can't see, I can hear a finger stirring. Business is business. Hold out your right hand. Boy, take his right hand by the wrist, and bring it near to my right!'

We both obeyed him to the letter, and I saw him pass something from the hollow of the hand that held his stick into the palm of the captain's, which closed upon it instantly.

'And now that's done,' said the blind man; and at the words he suddenly left hold of me, and, with incredible accuracy and nimbleness skipped out of the parlour and into the road, where, as I stood motionless, I could hear his stick go tap-tap-tapping into the distance.

It was some time before either I or the captain seemed to gather our senses; but at length, and about at the same moment, I released his wrist, which I was still holding, and he drew in his hand, and looked sharply into the palm.

'Ten o'clock!' he cried. 'Six hours. We'll do them yet'; and he sprang to his feet.

Even as he did so, he reeled, put his hand to his throat, stood swaying for a moment, and then, with a peculiar sound, fell from his whole height face foremost to the floor.

GEORGE MEREDITH

1828–1909

The Egoist

(First edition 1879)

CHAPTER V: CLARA MIDDLETON

[Sir Willoughby] looked the fittest; he justified the
dictum of Science. The survival of the Patternes was assured. 'I would', he said to his admirer, Mrs Mountstuart
Jenkinson, 'have bargained for health above everything,
but she has everything besides—lineage, beauty, breeding:
is what they call an heiress, and is the most accomplished
of her sex.' With a delicate art he conveyed to the lady's
understanding that Miss Middleton had been snatched
from a crowd, without a breath of the crowd having
offended his niceness. He did it through sarcasm at your
modern young women, who run about the world nibbling
and nibbled at, until they know one sex as well as the other,
and are not a whit less cognizant of the market than men;
pure, possibly; it is not so easy to say innocent; decidedly
not our feminine ideal. Miss Middleton was different: she
was the true ideal, fresh-gathered morning fruit in a basket,
warranted by her bloom.

Women do not defend their younger sisters for doing
what they perhaps have done—lifting a veil to be seen,
and peeping at a world where innocence is as poor a
guarantee as a babe's caul against shipwreck. Women of
the world never think of attacking the sensual stipulation

for perfect bloom, silver purity, which is redolent of the Oriental origin of the love-passion of their lords. Mrs Mountstuart congratulated Sir Willoughby on the prize he had won in the fair western-eastern.

'Let me see her,' she said; and Miss Middleton was introduced and critically observed.

She had the mouth that smiles in repose. The lips met full on the centre of the bow and thinned along to a lifting dimple; the eyelids also lifted slightly at the outer corners and seemed, like the lip into the limpid cheek, quickening up the temples, as with a run of light, or the ascension indicated off a shoot of colour. Her features were playfellows of one another, none of them pretending to rigid correctness, nor the nose to the ordinary dignity of governess among merry girls, despite which the nose was of a fair design, not acutely interrogative or inviting to gambols. Aspens imaged in water, waiting for the breeze, would offer a susceptible lover some suggestion of her face: a pure smooth-white face, tenderly flushed in the cheeks, where the gentle dints were faintly intermelting even during quietness. Her eyes were brown, set well between mild lids, often shadowed, not unwakeful. Her hair of lighter brown, swelling above her temples on the sweep to the knot, imposed the triangle of the fabulous wild woodland visage from brow to mouth and chin, evidently in agreement with her taste; and the triangle suited her; but her face was not significant of a tameless wildness or of weakness; her equable shut mouth threw its long curve to guard the small round chin from that effect; her eyes wavered only in humour, they were steady when thought-

fulness was awakened; and at such seasons the build of her
winter-beechwood hair lost the touch of nymph-like and
whimsical, and strangely, by mere outline, added to her
appearance of studious concentration. Observe the hawk
on stretched wings over the prey he spies, for an idea of
this change in the look of a young lady whom Vernon
Whitford could liken to the Mountain Echo, and Mrs
Mountstuart Jenkinson pronounced to be 'a dainty rogue
in porcelain'.

SAMUEL BUTLER
1835–1902

The Way of All Flesh
(First edition 1903)

CHAPTER XIII

FOR some time the pair said nothing: what they must have
felt during their first half-hour, the reader must guess, for
it is beyond my power to tell him; at the end of that time,
however, Theobald had rummaged up a conclusion from
some odd corner of his soul to the effect that now he and
Christina were married the sooner they fell into their
future mutual relations the better. If people who are in a
difficulty will only do the first little reasonable thing which
they can clearly recognise as reasonable, they will always
find the next step more easy both to see and take. What,
then, thought Theobald, was here at this moment the first
and most obvious matter to be considered, and what would
be an equitable view of his and Christina's relative posi-

tions in respect to it? Clearly their first dinner was their first joint entry into the duties and pleasures of married life. No less clearly it was Christina's duty to order it, and his own to eat it and pay for it.

The arguments leading to this conclusion, and the conclusion itself, flashed upon Theobald about three and a half miles after he had left Crampsford on the road to Newmarket. He had breakfasted early, but his usual appetite had failed him. They had left the vicarage at noon without staying for the wedding-breakfast. Theobald liked an early dinner; it dawned upon him that he was beginning to be hungry; from this to the conclusion stated in the preceding paragraph the steps had been easy. After a few minutes' further reflection he broached the matter to his bride, and thus the ice was broken.

Mrs Theobald was not prepared for so sudden an assumption of importance. Her nerves, never of the strongest, had been strung to their highest tension by the event of the morning. She wanted to escape observation; she was conscious of looking a little older than she quite liked to look as a bride who had been married that morning; she feared the landlady, the chambermaid, the waiter—everybody and everything; her heart beat so fast that she could hardly speak, much less go through the ordeal of ordering dinner in a strange hotel with a strange landlady. She begged and prayed to be let off. If Theobald would only order dinner this once, she would order it any day and every day in future.

But the inexorable Theobald was not to be put off with such absurd excuses. He was master now. Had not Christina less than two hours ago promised solemnly to honour and obey him, and was she turning restive over such a trifle as this? The loving smile departed from his face, and was succeeded by a scowl which that old Turk, his father, might have envied. 'Stuff and nonsense, my dearest Christina', he exclaimed mildly, and stamped his foot upon the floor of the carriage. 'It is a wife's duty to order her husband's dinner; you are my wife, and I shall expect you to order mine'. Theobald was nothing if he was not logical.

The bride began to cry, and said he was unkind; whereon he said nothing, but revolved unutterable things in his heart. Was this, then, the end of his six years of unflagging devotion? Was it for this that when Christina had offered to let him off he had stuck to his engagement? Was this the outcome of her talks about duty and spiritual-mindedness—that now upon the very day of her marriage she should fail to see that the first step in obedience to God lay in obedience to himself? He would drive back to Crampsford; he would complain to Mr and Mrs Allaby; he didn't mean to have married Christina; he hadn't married her; it was all a hideous dream; he would—But a voice kept ringing in his ears which said: 'YOU CAN'T, CAN'T, CAN'T.'

'CAN'T I?' screamed the unhappy creature to himself.

'No', said the remorseless voice, 'YOU CAN'T. YOU ARE A MARRIED MAN.'

He rolled back in his corner of the carriage and for the first time felt how iniquitous were the marriage laws of England.

COMMENTARY

PAGE 1

Sir Thomas Malory's *Morte d'Arthur* is an appropriate beginning to an anthology of modern English prose. It is in this book, and in Caxton's translations of French romances for the first printed books, that the rough attempts at English prose following the Norman Conquest were first shaped and polished. Little is known of the author, and it is only conjecture which connects him with Sir Thomas Malory of Newbold Revel in Warwickshire, who, after service in France with the Earl of Warwick, was imprisoned in 1451 and spent the rest of his life in prison.

The book purports to be a translation from the French, and was finished between 1469 and 1470. It is a sifting and arrangement of the mass of Arthurian legend, and combines the reign and death of King Arthur with stories of the quest of the Holy Grail, and the love of Sir Launcelot and Queen Guinevere. This episode takes place near the end of the book, following the dissolution of the Round Table, the death of Arthur, and Queen Guinevere's retirement into a nunnery. The style has lucidity and an unobtrusive balance of clause and sentence which yet does not retard the gentle flow of the narrative.

PAGE 3

The Chronicles of Froissart cover the period from 1323 to 1400. Though later historians have disproved many of the stories, Froissart's history was dependent upon oral testimony, and the picture of the period and of the last remnants of the chivalric tradition has great life and authenticity.

Lord Berners, who translated the book from the French, attended King Henry VIII at the Field of the Cloth of Gold. His narrative lacks the polish of Malory's prose, but its brisker style is well suited to the writing of his original. Malory was writing legend, Berners history. Malory's England was remote, indistinct, dreamlike; Berners's actual, highly coloured and authentic. This episode describes the surrender of the ill-fated King Richard II to Henry Bolingbroke, and, in the story of the greyhound, contains an element of pathos more rarely found in Berners than in Malory.

PAGE 6

Sir Thomas More's *Utopia,* originally written in Latin, is included because of its importance in the humanist thought of the Renaissance, rather than because of the literary merits of the translation. The author was a lawyer, a member of parliament and privy councillor in the reign of Henry VIII, until his refusal to countenance the king's divorce from Catherine of Aragon resulted in his indictment for high treason and his execution in 1535. He was a littérateur, critic and patron of art, and an intimate friend of Erasmus, who has left a description of More's cultivated Chelsea home.

Utopia was originally published in 1516 in Louvain, and in an English translation by Ralph Robynson in 1551. So immediate was its fame that Rabelais writing in 1546 makes a reference to 'Utopians'. Written partly in the form of an imaginary voyage, partly in the form of Plato's *Republic*, the book describes a land where communism is the natural law, property is forbidden, education is universal, and all religions are tolerated. The present passage describes the organisation of town and family life, in which cooking, eating, and the care of children are regarded as communal tasks.

PAGE 8

The imaginary voyage to an imaginary *Utopia* is balanced by one of the eye-witness accounts of actual voyages which form Richard Hakluyt's *Principal Navigations*. Richard Hakluyt was a clergyman and chaplain to Sir Edward Stafford, the English ambassador to Paris, from 1583–8. Irked by the reputation of the English for 'sluggish security', he began to collect accounts of English voyages of exploration, and these were first published in 1589. In recounting past achievements, he gave an impetus to further voyages and discoveries, and in 1598–1600 he published an enlarged edition which included accounts of the voyages of Raleigh, Gilbert, and the Cabots; of Frobisher's search for the north-west passage, and of Drake's circumnavigation of the globe.

Sir Humfrey Gilbert, in his second voyage here described, took possession of St John's and the adjacent parts of Newfoundland, but his ship was lost on the voyage home to England. Written in most cases by eye-witnesses the prose in these accounts is sometimes involved and obscure, but often breaks into passages of great simplicity and vividness.

PAGE 11

As in other countries, the Renaissance in England brought about a renewed interest in classical authors, and a spate of translations. Many of these by virtue of their style have become classics in their own right: in poetry notably Chapman's *Homer* and Golding's *Ovid,* and in prose Florio's *Montaigne,* and North's *Plutarch's Lives.* In many cases the translations were made through the intermediary of another modern language, and North translated not the original Greek, but the French version of Jacques Amyot.

So clear and unaffected is North's prose, so precise and vivid are his descriptions, to such effect does he embroider his original text, that his stories have the ring of an original creation and none of the marks of a translation. Shakespeare drew many of his plots from North, and this description of Cleopatra in her barge can be found with very little alteration of rhythm or word in *Antony and Cleopatra.*

PAGE 13

Sir Philip Sidney embodied in himself the ideal virtues of the Renaissance gentleman; he was a poet and novelist, a man of considerable learning and scholarship, and at the same time a soldier and man of action, killed in the relief of Zutphen in 1586. *The Apologie for Poetrie* was provoked by Gosson's *The School of Abuse* which condemned 'such peevish cattle as poets and pipers'. In indignant and eloquent prose, Sidney sets forth his conception of the poet as the *vates,* the diviner or prophet, superior both to the philosopher and the historian: 'Of all Sciences ... is our Poet the Monarch.' Not only does he defend the poet, but he defines his functions, condemns the formlessness of much of the writing of his time, insists upon the importance of the dramatic unities, and finally ends a considerable piece of literary criticism by invoking all the deities of his literary pantheon to condemn in a mannered malediction all who 'laugh at the name of poets'.

PAGE 16

The two passages from early Elizabethan novels form a pointed contrast to one another, and partially typify two of the many strains which make up the English novel of later centuries.

In his *Euphues* and *Euphues and his England,* Lyly evolved an extreme form of the poetic prose which is found also in such novels as Lodge's *Rosalind* and Sidney's *Arcadia*. His two books are of little interest for their characterisation, or for their plots, which are tenuous tales of the adventures of Euphues and his friend Philautus in Rome and London; they are interesting chiefly in their style, which had a widespread effect on later prose, and which gave a new word to the language: *euphuism,* to describe an affected manner of writing.

The style is based on an elaborated balance of clause with clause pointed by alliteration. The present passage, describing an English girl whom Euphues met, is full of examples. It is interesting to compare this antithetical style with that of Gibbon in the eighteenth century. A second characteristic is the use of allusions to historical and

mythological personages, which in this passage is typi-
fied by the reference to Queen Elizabeth as *Vesta* and *Diana*,
and to her court as vestal virgins.

PAGE 18

By contrast, Nashe's *The Unfortunate Traveller,* the first picaresque novel in English, is a robust and satirical story of the
adventures of one Jacke Wilton, a page in the reign of
Henry VIII. His adventures take him to Flanders, Germany,
and Italy; he takes part in battles, sieges and massacres.
Later, as page to the Earl of Surrey, the lover of the fair
Geraldine, he accompanies him to Italy, where the present
episode takes place on the occasion of their wrongful
imprisonment. After a grotesque description of the mingled
savagery and civilisation of Renaissance Italy, he marries a
courtesan and is last seen in the camp of Henry VIII at the
Field of the Cloth of Gold.

   Nashe was not only the creator of a new genre in English,
the picaresque novel, but also of a new style. His prose is
swift and spare, by contrast with Lyly's, and through it
runs the note of satire and mocking irony which he used
with such effect in his savage pamphlets against the Government of the day. In this novel, the characterisation is rarely
profound, but he has a shrewd understanding of the
essentials of personality, and an eye quick to seize upon
physical beauty and idiosyncrasy.

PAGE 20

   English was to Francis Bacon as to Thomas More a
secondary language. His chief philosophical and didactic

works are written in Latin. Perhaps for this reason his English prose has great compression and intensity, and words are often used with all the weight of their Latin derivation. Using subtle variations of rhythm, he pointed his arguments with vivid similes and poetic images, and many phrases and epigrams from his *Essays* have entered into common use. In the breadth of his intellect, in the range of his knowledge, and in his interest in science, he was a typical man of the Renaissance, and is amongst the pioneers of philosophic and scientific thought. Unfortunately he is also remembered for his treachery towards his friend the Earl of Essex and for his conviction for 'corruption and neglect' when he was Lord Chancellor to James I. Pope described him as 'the wisest, brightest and meanest of mankind'.

PAGE 22

It is difficult to over-emphasise the importance of the authorised translation of the Bible in the history of English literature. Within the compass of one book a wealth of legends, myths, stories, poetry, wisdom and mysticism, was made available in the native tongue and thereby enriched the imagination of the whole people. Since 1611, passages from the Bible have been read aloud in all church services until its phrases have entered everyday speech to such an extent that it is with a shock of surprise that they are rediscovered in their original context. Through the ear their cadences and rhythms have been deeply and often unconsciously absorbed, and reappear in later prose, notably in religious and mystic writings. Perhaps the most remarkable thing about the prose is its flexibility: in narrative, it is simple, homely, sometimes harsh; yet it can comprehend the mysticism of the Apocalypse, the succinct wisdom of the Proverbs, and often attains the rhythms of blank verse and the intensity of poetry, particularly in the Psalms. Many of its effects are gained by the subtle interplay of short English words and sonorous words of Latin derivation, and by the variations of pace and rhythm.

This version was the work of forty-seven scholars appointed by James I to reconsider and revise the earlier translations of Tyndale and Wycliffe. Their final version is largely based upon Tyndale's translation made in 1530, so that the language and turns of phrase had even at that time a slightly archaic flavour. Later scholars have complained that the Authorised Version often confuses the text by inaccurate translation, but revised versions have failed to oust it in general popularity.

PAGE 24

Death often came suddenly to men of the seventeenth century; and a morbid fascination with the trappings of death pervades their writing. In the sermons of Donne and Jeremy Taylor, in the prose of Dekker and Sir Thomas Browne, worms and winding-sheets impinge on meditations on mortality and death. Dekker's baroque description of the plague year of 1603 is an epitome of this carnival of mortality. He describes the plague in an allegory of Death encamped with his army in the outskirts of the plague-ridden city, but relieves the gloom of his account with anecdotes of its effect on the citizens of London.

Dekker was born and lived for most of his life in London, whose life he depicted so humorously in his comedies and in the *Guls Hornbooke* in which Elizabethan London and its people come alive. The hyperbole and rhythmic effects sometimes tend to overreach themselves and to verge on parody, but one is conscious as in all Jacobean writing of the freshness of language, and of a rich and expanding vocabulary.

PAGE 26

'A preacher in earnest . . . always preaching to himself like an Angel from a cloud, but in none.' Thus Izaak Walton described John Donne, the metaphysical poet, rake and wit who ended his life as Dean of St Paul's, and was one of the most eloquent preachers of all time.

Donne wrote down his sermons after delivery, using his own system of punctuation to reveal the emphasis, pace and modulations of his voice. This makes it easy to imagine the eloquence of the mounting curves of his argument, an eloquence carefully contrived, as in all great oratory, to give an effect of impassioned spontaneity. The idea of sin, breaking the communion between man and God, particularly moved him both in his sermons and his poetry; and all his poetic resources of imagery and vocabulary are used to make his writing rich and yet fresh.

PAGE 28

Burton confessed to writing his *Anatomy* as a cure for his own distemper. It has certainly been an antidote against melancholy ever since. From his book he appears as the reverse of a melancholic man, though he lived 'a silent, sedentary, private life, *mihi et musis* in the University'. Sitting in his rooms in Christ Church, amongst his library of some 2000 books, he gathered from them his examples of the vagaries of the human mind to make a ragbag of quotation, anecdote and comment, a book of half-a-million words.

There is no species of melancholy which he does not diagnose or for which he does not specify a cure: among them amorous 'dotage', here described. As he could discard no anecdote which appeared to illustrate his points, so he could omit no word of which he enjoyed the sound or savour. Discursive, witty and ironic, he was a delight to Dr Johnson, an exemplar to Sterne, and favourite reading for both Keats and Lamb.

PAGE 31

As melancholy is the least part of Burton's book, so fishing is not the whole of the *Compleat Angler*. It has been the delight of people who have never handled a rod. It takes the form of a dialogue between *Venator* (a hunter) and *Piscator* (a fisherman) in which the latter commends his own craft and gives directions for catching fresh-water fish and dressing them for the table. The dialogues are interspersed with songs and poems, and the prose has the leisurely movement of a long summer afternoon.

In his life Izaak Walton spanned the century. He was a friend and parishioner of John Donne, was the fishing companion of Sir Henry Wotton, and wrote both their biographies, yet he lived to see the Restoration and most of the reign of Charles II.

PAGE 33

Meditations on the death of the body and the immortality of the soul fill the religious writing of the century. To guide the devotions of Lady Carbery of Golden Grove to whom he was domestic chaplain, Jeremy Taylor wrote his rules of *Holy Living* and *Holy Dying*. He had retired to Golden Grove after being taken prisoner at the Royalist defeat in Cardigan, and remained there until the restoration of Charles II, when he was made Bishop of Down and Connor. As a preacher, he was second only to Donne in eloquence.

The music of his prose varies from simplicity to rich audacity, with metaphors and similes elaborated to the furthest degree of imagination. Combined with this is a power of precise description and poetic vision which has won him the name of the 'Shakespeare of Divines'.

PAGE 35

'What song the Sirens sang, or what name Achilles assumed when he hid among women.' This famous speculation of Sir Thomas Browne's is typical of his thinking. A doctor by profession, he was by nature a mystic. His Anglican faith is accompanied by wide reading in the classics, his interest in science tempered by superstitious beliefs in magic, astrology and witchcraft. This ambivalence is apparent in all his writing, particularly in his longest book, *Pseudodoxia epidemica*, ostensibly written to refute current superstitions.

Urn Burial was inspired by the discovery of some fifty ancient burial urns in a field in Norfolk. Its theme is the vanity of human glory compared with 'the metaphysics of true belief'. Ranging through his wide knowledge of ancient customs of burial and disposal of the dead, he cites many classical examples to show that there is little hope of survival in the memory of man. No writer had such an ear for the sonorities of prose. Rich with metaphor and allusion, his style is musically as disciplined as verse, if occasionally marred by too great latinity.

PAGE 37

The Civil War was more than a political conflict; it brought with it many changes in modes of thought and methods of writing. Thought became controversial and polemic; for the first time an attempt was made to write current history, to explain through historical fact the controversies of the war. Both Puritans and Royalists employed writers as polemists, but Milton was the only one whose pamphlets have, by stating the larger issues of the conflict, outlived the occasion for which they were written.

By choice a poet, Milton wrote little or no poetry for twenty years during the war. Instead he descended into what he called 'the cool element of prose'. Cool Milton rarely was, even in prose, and the poet breaks through in the rhetoric, in similes and imagery. Often he turns his attack against his own side, and here denounces a proposal for censorship of books by the state, which he sees as a reversion to the customs of the papacy. He regards promiscuous reading as essential to thought and learning, and to the health of a vital and enfranchised nation.

PAGE 40

Milton's impassioned pleading contrasts with the objectivity of the royalist Lord Clarendon, who followed the Prince of Wales into exile and there began to write his *History of the Great Rebellion*. Though broadly planned and handled with skill in its combination of detail and easy narrative, the history is perhaps surpassed by his portraits of the main protagonists in the war. Based on the portrait or 'character' then in fashion in France, his sketches probe motive and action, but without rancour and with great tolerance. The Marquis of Montrose was a great Royalist general executed by the Covenanters in 1650.

Though Clarendon's writing is sometimes jerky, it moves in the direction of a new style, the style of scientific thought and rational analysis. The involved periods of Browne and Taylor have disappeared, and even the writing of mystics such as Bunyan and Traherne is couched in simple language and brief sentences.

PAGE 42

The Pilgrim's Progress is probably the greatest religious allegory in English. Bunyan, a tinker and a man of small education, began to write his book when in prison for preaching without a licence. The allegory takes the form of a dream in which the author follows Christian on his journey towards the Celestial City, describes the fiends and giants whom he overcomes and the personages such as Mr Worldly Wiseman, Faithful and Hope whom he meets on the way. In the second part, Christian's wife Christiana, sets out on the same journey with her children, escorted by Mr Great-heart, who protects them against Giant Despair and other monsters, and raises their spirits in the Valley of the Shadow of Death, here described.

To depict the life of man as a journey is a commonplace of allegory, but here it moves within the framework of a well-told tale of adventure still widely read as a story. Hope and Faithful, Mr Great-heart and Giant Despair, indeed all the personages who represent the follies, virtues and vices of man, are real people, shrewdly observed and described; the landscape of the mind through which they move is real country. In this passage the solid reality of the child and his mother throws into relief the gloom and the darkness, the fire and the mist; the fiend upon the road is realised by means of the dialogue between Christiana and her son, and gains in effect by the lack of direct description.

PAGE 45

In Bunyan there is always an awareness of two levels, of the eternal transmuting everyday existence, but it is in Traherne that the mystic element in seventeenth-century writing reaches its highest point. The childlike sense of wonder whose loss he mourns in this passage is nevertheless the vision which informs the whole of his writing, and he is probably the most transcendental of the English mystics.

Little is known of the externals of his life, except that he was the son of a shoemaker, that he was sent to Oxford by a benefactor, became a parish priest and eventually a private chaplain. He died at the age of thirty-seven. Mystery also attends the manuscripts of his poems and of the

Centuries of Meditations. They were bequeathed to his brother and disappeared for many years until found and published by Bertram Dobell in 1908. The *Meditations,* true to their name, reveal no ordered system of thought. They are prose poems imbued with a poetic vision of the world, written in a simple melodious style with enchanting imagery.

PAGE 48

From the testament of the mystic to the diary of the gossip. No man has recorded the minutiae of his daily life as did Samuel Pepys, Secretary to the Navy of Charles II. Naïve and shrewd, vain and frivolous, philanderer and philosopher, he was a musician who liked to take his part in madrigals, a connoisseur of painting and prints, and, as befitted the President of the Royal Society, interested in the 'instrument for perspective made by Dr Wren'.

He kept his diary, written in cipher and not intended for publication, from 1660 until 1669, when failing eyesight forced him to abandon it. The man and his style cannot be separated: self-revealing but unselfconscious, desultory and yet expressive, his diary throws a brilliant if fitful light on the background of the court and political life of the Restoration.

PAGE 50

To John Aubrey we owe a great many of the anecdotes which enliven the history of the past. He started to compile his 'lives' at the instigation of Anthony à Wood, an Oxford historian who was working on biographies of Oxford writers and bishops. Their collaboration continued for twenty-five years until Wood was expelled from the University for a supposed libel on the Earl of Clarendon.

Aubrey, shiftless, often in debt, had a wide circle of acquaintance in London and the country, was a member of the Royal Society, and an antiquarian and historian. But above all he was a gossip with an eye for lively detail and an inimitable method of expression. 'My head was alwaies working; never idle, and even travelling (which from 1649 until 1670 was never off horseback) did gleane some observations, of which I have a collection in folio of two quiers of paper plus a dust basket, some whereof are to be valued.' Much of the material he gathered was unsifted and he often repeats or contradicts himself. He was rarely capable of sustained writing, but no biographer has so condensed the whole of a man's character, appearance and habits into a 'brief life'.

PAGE 52

The rationalism of Restoration thought is apparent also in literary criticism. In Dryden's *Essay of Dramatick Poesy* is found for the first time an attempt at detailed criticism of dramatic writing. The essay is in the form of a conversation between four friends who discuss the merits of various types of drama: classical, contemporary French and Elizabethan. They debate the necessity for the unities, and the merits of verse and prose in plays.

Dryden was himself a considerable dramatist and poet. There can be no greater contrast than that between his writing and that of Sir Philip Sidney in his *Apologie for Poetrie*. Analysis demands simplicity and economy; the sentences are short and precise, the long period and rhetorical peroration have disappeared. The writing is elegant and the ideas emerge with ease and clarity. *Neander*, who speaks here, was probably intended to represent Dryden himself, and his tribute to Shakespeare is the first rather muted note in what was to become in later centuries a chorus of adulation.

PAGE 55

Chronological order has here been violated in order to contrast the criticism of the late eighteenth century with that of the Restoration. Though Dr Johnson makes an effort to establish literary principles, his criticism is in the main as empirical as that of Dryden, rejecting any pedantry such as an attempt to apply the rules of the unities to Shakespeare.

The son of a bookseller, he spent a short time at Oxford, became a schoolmaster, and eventually came to London to seek his fortune as an author. Penury for a great many years resulted, though he wrote for the *Gentleman's Magazine*, edited *The Idler* and *The Rambler*, wrote poems, a play and a novel. For eight years he worked on his Dictionary, and edited an edition of Shakespeare. His life eased in 1762 when he received a government pension, and in the following year met Boswell, his biographer, and became the centre of a circle including Garrick, Goldsmith and Reynolds.

Though perhaps his personality counts for more than his literary output, he was a great critic, who distrusted innovations, but sought for some acceptable criteria for judging past writers. His *Lives of the Poets* were intended as biographical and critical prefaces to an edition of the

English poets, but they were eventually published separately, and consist of the lives of fifty-two poets dating from Cowley. It is interesting to compare the mannered style of his writing with the simplicity of Dryden, and amusing to notice the difference between the rhetoric of his written style and the wit and easy improvisation of his conversation.

PAGE 57

More Protean even than Johnson in his writing, Defoe was a turncoat in politics, and in his life a jack-of-all-trades: merchant, traveller, soldier first for Monmouth, then for William of Orange, secret agent for both Tories and Whigs, on several occasions imprisoned, and once pilloried. In writing: journalist, pamphleteer, novelist, historian and poet, leaving behind him at least 250 works. Facts were his raw material. In his creative writing and particularly in his novels, he used them to mould his figures into solidity and life through an accumulation of the detail of their lives. Though his method was akin to journalism, his characters, Moll Flanders and Colonel Jack, Roxana and Captain Singleton, are nevertheless great imaginative creations emerging in all their solid reality from the mêlée of eighteenth-century life. In his pictures of low life he harks back to Dekker and in his use of imaginatively realised detail forward to the historical method of Carlyle.

His *Life of Colonel Jack* is a picaresque tale of a boy deserted by his parents, who becomes a pickpocket and later a soldier. Kidnapped and sent to Virginia as a slave, he becomes an overseer and finally a rich planter. He returns to

England to a series of unfortunate matrimonial adventures, but in keeping with the moralising strain running through Defoe's racy and humorous tales, he finally repents and dies in prosperity. No part of the book is more vivid than the picture of the life of an innocent boy amongst the thieves and pickpockets of London, from which this passage is taken.

PAGE 59

In the way that a man often matches his time, in the period of religious and intellectual controversy at the beginning of the eighteenth century emerged Swift, one of the most savage satirists and finished ironists in any language. In his attacks on false intellectual values, on oppression and social injustice, and even on the faults of the Church in which he took orders, he employed every form of writing: allegory in *Gulliver's Travels* and *A Tale of a Tub*; poetry, pamphlets and tracts. Cerebral illness afflicted him during the whole of his life, causing melancholy and, in the later part of his life, insanity.

It is difficult to define briefly the nature of his irony. It is not by chance that *Gulliver's Travels* is most often read as a children's story, for it has the merits of a fairy tale: action, pace, and above all the fertile invention of concrete detail to domesticate the fantasy. These are also some of the ingredients of successful irony. The method is twofold: to describe an ideal form of life and by implication and paradox to attack the real; and the reverse method which he more frequently used in his pamphlets and satires. He describes the wrong-headed, the horrific, the lewd, the cruel, or the merely stupid, as though they were ideals not yet attained, but still to be striven for. But so logical is the thought, so easy the progression of ideas, so calmly persuasive the writing, that the final ironic reversal is often delayed by the lulled acceptance of the reader. More than any other factor, it is his style which achieves this. Supple and lucid, it can move without effort from simple narrative to subtly ironic statement and argument.

A Tale of a Tub is a satire directed against the three official churches, but its chief interest now lies in the ironic digressions interspersed in the narrative, on madness, on critics, and as here, a digression upon digressions.

PAGE 62

Swift was greater than his age, Addison and Steele were of their time, the time of conversation in coffee-houses, of the introduction of newspapers, and the upsurge of a sentimental middle-class culture. The growth of the Whig party and the invasion of politics by rich merchant families began to change the aspect of writing. For the first time literature treated man as a social being, within the hierarchy of close-bound ties. A new moralising strain sought to direct him towards the strengthening of family affection and the purifying of morals in human relationships.

The Spectator, which appeared daily for nearly two years, was in no sense a paper devoted to current events; instead Steele, Addison and other writers gave advice on morals, manners and the good life. The paper purported to be conducted by a small club, the principal member being Sir Roger de Coverley, an idealised country squire. In him appears for the first time the character of the whimsical innocent, often overcome by harsh society, but finally triumphant by virtue of his simplicity. He was to have many imitators in later novels.

Contributions included essays, imaginary letters and character sketches of Sir Roger de Coverley and his circle. The best of the ironic essays were written by Addison, a classical scholar, poet, dramatist and politician, who ended his life as Secretary of State. His irony is much less savage than that of Swift, and his thought is harmoniously contained in the compass of the essay, a form which he uses with great skill.

Steele's contributions are written to a looser pattern than the more tightly constructed and reasoned essays of Addison, and many of the character sketches of Sir Roger are written by him. Spending his youth in the army, he led a dissipated life, wrote a number of sentimental comedies, and then to make money, turned to periodicals: *The Tatler, The Spectator,* and a number of other journals which successively failed after a short period. Nevertheless, in *The Spectator,* the playful moralising, the elegance and the half-tone irony, appear as new elements in English writing, largely introduced by Steele and perfected by Addison.

PAGE 67

Clarissa is almost certainly the longest novel in the English language. Prolix it must inevitably be, for it is written in the form of letters, not from a single observer, but from nearly all the characters. The novelist moves as though round the periphery of a circle, projecting numerous radii towards the central incidents. It is almost a novel in kaleidoscope. Richardson, a man of simple education, was a printer. He compiled a series of model letters for a 'complete letter-writer' and this led to his first novel, *Pamela*, written in this form.

Clarissa was published in five volumes over a period of two years, and readers of sensibility all over Europe avidly followed her adventures and mourned her death, which was protracted for nearly the whole of one volume. Lovelace, the villain-hero of the story, elopes with Clarissa, a girl of gentle breeding, against the wishes of her parents. After a series of adventures, Clarissa in the lodgings of Mrs Sinclair is drugged and ravished by Lovelace, and taking leave of her senses writes a series of mad letters; part of one is here given. Managing to escape, she is wrongfully arrested, is eventually released, and after an unsuccessful attempt at reconcilement with her family, dies. Lovelace, delirious, ill and repentant, is pursued to Paris by her cousin Colonel Warden and killed in a duel.

If Rubens is a painter's painter, Richardson is a novelist's novelist in the variety of his styles. Lovelace, the satanic Lovelace, at times witty and sardonic, at others repentant and pleading with the adamant Clarissa, is one of the most fully realised male characters in fiction. Anna Howe, practical and teasing, Clarissa's solid uncles, the fluttering mother, the solid prosy Belford, all emerge from their letters, and in comparison Clarissa in her unyielding resistance is occasionally wearisome. But in this delirious letter, the mad logic, the surrealist juxtapositions, the sudden transitions of mood which make up madness, are brilliantly realised, and bear comparison with Shakespeare's mad scenes. In an earlier letter of Lovelace's, there is a horrific picture of Mrs Sinclair, whom Clarissa fears: 'The old dragon straddled up to her, with her arms kemboed again, her eyebrows erect like the bristles upon a hog's back, and scowling over her shortened nose, more than half hid her ferret eyes.'

PAGE 70

It was the pathos, the sentiment and the prolixity of Richardson which made Fielding write his first novel. Unlike Richardson he came of an aristocratic family, was a barrister, and had already written a number of comedies before, provoked by the publication of *Pamela,* he wrote a parody of it in *Joseph Andrews.* Later he took up political journalism, became a justice of the peace, and wrote three more novels before his somewhat early death.

More than any other novelist he set the example for later novels, for their form, their tone, and their characters. His work in the theatre had taught him economy and speed, and though *Tom Jones* is in many ways a picaresque novel, it abandons the method of flat continuity and straightforward narrative, and moves the hero in rapid transition through a series of comic set pieces, full of racy dialogue. Tom Jones, a foundling, high-spirited and generous, and adopted by a wealthy benefactor Mr Allworthy, falls in love with Sophia, daughter of a fox-hunting squire. By the machinations of his tutor and Blifil, a classic sneak, he is driven out in company with a schoolmaster, and falls in with a series of adventures, many of them amorous. Sophia runs away to join him, pursued by Squire Western. Tom is discovered to be the son of Allworthy's sister, and all ends in this scene of reconciliation.

The inwardness of characters was Richardson's greatest concern; Fielding penetrates as acutely from the social being inwards, and builds up his characters by means of action and the richly characterised dialogue of which he is a master. Sophia, 'a parcel of maidenish tricks', Lady Bellaston, the amorous harridan, Western, the hunting squire, the high-minded Allworthy; none of them are stock characters, and the imitations of them which appear in later novels rarely attained to the acuteness of Fielding's insight. Basically Fielding is a social reformer, a reformer by ridicule of some of the barbarities of English life of which he saw too much as a London magistrate; each section of *Tom Jones* is prefaced by a moral essay. Richardson's subtle analysis, often prolonged to delay the action, is not a trait found again in the English novel until the twentieth century, but Fielding's realistic method was and still seems to be the fictional form most happily suited to the English temperament.

PAGE 72

Fielding died on a voyage to Lisbon and is buried there. Like many other writers of the century, Smollett crossed the channel and wrote a book of his experiences. From his *Travels in France and Italy,* emerges a self-portrait of the man himself in his middle age, ill, testy, disappointed, but still responsive to new experiences. As a young man he had sailed as a ship's surgeon to the West Indies; his adventures on this voyage provided him with material for *Roderick Random,* his first novel, and with the chief comic character in *Peregrine Pickle*: the old sea dog still using the jargon of his profession, as unhappy on shore as a landed fish, Commodore Trunnion, with his fear of women and hatred of lawyers, living in the country protected by a 'garrison' of a one-legged lieutenant and his boatswain Tom Pipes.

Smollett could rough out the essentials of a character, the eccentricities of speech and appearance, with as much economy and speed as the caricaturists Rowlandson and Cruikshank who were to illustrate his books. But as with the other great creator of eccentrics, Dickens, his characters rarely grow. Coarse and splenetic, more virulent in his satire than Fielding, Smollett is a man with a grudge against society, but he writes with speed, zest and a relish for crude comedy.

PAGE 75

It has been thought that Sterne owes the characters of Uncle Toby and Corporal Trim in *Tristram Shandy* to the example of Smollett. Whatever truth there may be in this, *Tristram Shandy* is in most ways the most personal and original of books. Sterne made a cult of eccentricity. His pages are spattered with asterisks, the punctuation is unique in the varying lengths of the dashes, some pages are black, others marbled, others quite blank. The book contains none of the opinions, and very little of the life of the nominal hero.

Time was an element which Sterne freely maltreated; he cut it, reversed it, doubled back. In his use of flash-back and stream of consciousness he is surprisingly modern. What plot the book has is mainly concerned with peevish and eccentric Walter Shandy, Tristram's father, and his brother, Uncle Toby, and his servant Corporal Trim. But the action is freely held up by long digressions, and the book appeared in nine volumes over seven years.

Though a clergyman in orders, Sterne spent many years in France, and his marriage was disrupted by his 'small quiet attentions' to various women. In him coarseness became a sentimental pruriency, but he could write uproarious comic scenes, though the characters are nearly always Sterne's *personae* mouthing and winking behind the masks. It is a nonsensical, maddening, delightful book.

PAGE 78

James Boswell, 'Scottish squirelet' and comic-opera revolutionary, found a vocation for twenty years in devoted discipleship to Dr Johnson. For twenty years he listened to the rumblings, the lightnings, the wit, the paradoxes and the epigrams. And for seven years, with an acute ear for the rhythms and intonations of talk, he recorded it all to re-create his prophet of Bolt Court; and with him, the other men of intellectual London who revolved about him: Garrick, Reynolds and Goldsmith, Burke, Wilkes and Charles James Fox. Perhaps no other biography has this immediacy, this sense of involvement in events. Certainly no man's conversation has before or since been recorded with such accuracy and verve.

PAGE 80

No lively letter-writer can be wholly free of innocent exhibitionism. In Horace Walpole it is combined with wit, gaiety, and a sometimes malicious interest in men and affairs; in the idiocies of politics—he was a member of parliament and the son of Sir Robert Walpole—and in the *longueurs* of polite society which he both cherished and mocked. An eighteenth-century Aubrey, interested in painting and antiquities, he travelled all over England to discover and describe medieval buildings, and in the first flush of the Gothic revival, transformed his house Strawberry Hill into 'a little Gothick castle', and wrote 'a Gothick story', *The Castle of Otranto*.

And from his little Gothic castle streamed letter after letter, to Sir Horace Mann, to the Countess of Ossory, to George Montague and Madame du Deffand. Amusing, affectionate, intimate and shrewd, they give a lively picture of eighteenth-century life.

PAGE 83

'Mrs Montagu, the literary lady . . . bound up Mr Gibbon's history without the last two offensive chapters.' When the first volume of the *Decline and Fall* appeared in 1776, it provoked a great deal of criticism by its ironic treatment of early Christian orthodoxy. Gibbon saw the growth of Christianity as a political as well as a moral force in the decline and degeneracy of the Roman world. For the first time an attempt had been made to discover the movement of history and the influence of thought and spiritual forces upon it, and Gibbon's account straddles between the antique and the modern world, from the age of Trajan to the fall of Constantinople in 1453.

Gibbon, born a Protestant, was converted to Catholicism at the age of sixteen, but a few years later reverted to Protestantism. On the grand tour, 'musing among the ruins of the Capitol', he conceived the idea of writing of the fall of the Roman civilisation, a project which it took him over twenty years to complete. Though later research has established facts unknown to him, the scope of his history and his powers of re-creating the life of Rome and Byzantium have never been surpassed. His antithetical style with its elaborate yoking of clauses and the underlying irony is unmistakably his and at the same time the hall-mark of the late eighteenth century.

PAGE 85

While Gibbon was writing of the fall of the Roman Empire, the storm which brought down the French monarchy had blown up across the Channel. Burke's treatise was provoked by a sermon in vindication of the French Revolution preached by Dr Price. In reply Burke attacked the motives and characters of the revolutionaries, denied their assertion of the 'rights of man', and concluded with a plea for the reform and not the destruction of the old regime. At the time the French royal family was still in custody in Paris, and Burke was not to know that the king and queen would be executed in 1793.

Burke was an Irishman, a member of the Whig party and one of the most eloquent orators in the House of Commons, speaking always in defence of emancipation and reform. But he remained an implacable enemy of French jacobinism, and broke away from Fox and the rest of the Whig party on this issue. The House of Commons of this period produced a crop of notable orators, amongst them Sheridan, Pitt and Charles James Fox. The issues which they fought over were part of the whole movement of political theory towards liberalism and reform, but Burke probably expressed the sentiments of the greater part of the English people in his conception of society as an organic growth not to be broken by anarchy or violent revolution. The styles of his public speeches and his political pamphlets are almost identical: reason is relieved by pathos, logic by sentiment, and the whole cadenced for the voice and decorated with imagery.

PAGE 87

Emma was published soon after the Battle of Waterloo, but not one reference to the Napoleonic wars appears in all its pages. Instead Jane Austen's genius lay in her concentration on the life which she knew and understood, the life of the rural middle-class, the squires, clergymen, militia, and shopkeepers in the villages and small county towns where she spent her life. It was life seen through the wrong end of a telescope: in miniature and very clear. More purely classical than any other English novelist in her freedom from moral obsessions, she understood the interplay of relationships in small communities, and saw with a clear eye the urges of vanity and self-love, and the dangers of pride and self-deception.

Her plots centre round the fate of her women characters

in the marriage game, a new angle of approach which had begun with Fanny Burney, and which produced the later English domestic novel. Perhaps her most shrewdly observed and developed character, Emma Woodhouse, is a self-deceiving and somewhat self-satisfied young woman who, seeking to direct the life of a young protégée, Harriet Smith, tries to achieve a marriage between her and the vicar, Mr Elton, only to find that Mr Elton aspires to her own hand. When this is refused, he becomes betrothed to Miss Hawkins, an heiress, and Emma is further humiliated in her match-making before she marries Mr Knightley, with whom she has unwittingly been in love.

Jane Austen understood the feminine temperament better than the male, though she could create richly comic characters of either sex, particularly in the eccentricities of their conversation. Her own personality rarely obtrudes itself, except in the power of her dispassionate irony.

PAGE 90

Scott's writing room in Edinburgh looked up towards the Castle Rock towering above the town. From the Castle to Holyrood runs the Royal Mile where the gloomy Tolbooth prison known as the 'Heart of Mid-Lothian' was being demolished in the year in which he wrote the book. It was this prison that was invaded by the mob which carried off Captain Porteous to hang him; he had been condemned to death for firing on the mob in a previous riot and later reprieved. In the novel this is combined with the story of Effie Deans also condemned to death for the murder of her child, and saved by her sister Jeannie who, refusing to lie on her sister's behalf goes to London to gain a reprieve from Queen Caroline.

Scott has been accused of failing to understand the feminine temperament, but this is true only of his aristocratic women. He understood the peasant women who were his servants, and Jeannie and Effie were peasants. It is always the country people and the townsfolk who live most vividly in his novels, and *The Heart of Mid-Lothian* is full of them: thieves, cranks, fanatics, and scores of simple homely bodies thronging the narrow wynds and streets of Edinburgh. Scott could create dramatic scenes, described with a mastery of narrative, effortless, fast-moving, yet embracing small details without slowing the action. It is this power of story-telling which still helps to carry one through the twenty-odd volumes of the Waverley Novels, to bear with the idealised men and women and their stilted conversation, and which enables the great comic scenes to ride over the long doric dialogues; this even more than his sense of history.

Trained as a lawyer, he made his reputation as a poet, before entering into partnership in a bookselling business. The novels were published anonymously for thirteen years before he acknowledged their authorship. Near the end of his life, he became involved in the failure of his business, and shortened his life in an effort to meet his creditors.

PAGE 92

The writers of the romantic movement liked to write about themselves and about each other. In a period which made a cult of the intensification of emotional life, of imagination and sensibility rather than intelligence, self-analysis was both a fashion and a habit of mind. In confessions, in autobiography—literary or amorous, in prose or in verse—in letters and essays, they poured it out. One of the most remarkable books of this kind is Hazlitt's *Liber Amoris,* the story of his love for the daughter of his landlady. It is remarkable because it combines Hazlitt's blind self-immolation and his ironic analysis of what he knew to be a sentimental illusion. It is this duality which makes his literary criticism both lively and penetrating.

Starting life as a painter, he then turned to journalism and literary criticism, and though to some extent he stood aloof from the life of his time, a number of the writers of the period were his friends. In his *Spirit of the Age* he made assessments of his contemporaries, but no essay is so immediate as this description of the two young poets, Coleridge and Wordsworth, with their different habits of composing and reciting their verses.

PAGE 95

Shelley had a more poetic and intuitive vision of Coleridge:

> he who sits obscure
> In the exceeding lustre and the pure
> Intense irradiation of a mind,
> With its own internal lightning blind . . . .

Coleridge penetrated more deeply into the nature of artistic creation than any critic before him had done. He understood the tensions underlying the writing of poetry and its projection into the mind of the reader. With a mind which ranged over every aspect of knowledge, 'a library cormorant' as he called himself, he is one of the greatest interpreters of Shakespeare and of Wordsworth.

In *Biographia Literaria* his ideas are often embedded in accounts of the German philosophers and autobiographical detail, but they are well worth the search. Poets are often the best critics of poetry; Coleridge is one of the greatest of them.

PAGE 97

Shakespeare was the lodestone of the romantic poets. For Keats he possessed the attribute of 'negative capability', an attribute which he considered essential for poets and which he describes in the present letter: 'the poet has none; no identity . . .' Delighting to be 'the chameleon poet', not 'the virtuous philosopher', Keats wrote no essays or literary criticism, but threw off ideas about poetry and the imaginative life in the course of letters to his family and friends. Often their epigrammatic quality has the power of Blake's aphorisms to set up reverberations in the mind. No poet has left behind a comparable series of letters to illumine his poems, or such revealing and impassioned love letters as those he wrote to Fanny Brawne before his early death.

PAGE 100

In the hands of Charles Lamb the essay lost for ever the detachment and impersonality of the eighteenth century, and reverted to the intimacy of Montaigne. To this end his style is most carefully contrived. Behind the mask of Elia he uses every trick of rhetoric, every mannerism of style to buttonhole the reader. Of his own genuine warmth and charm his letters are a testimony, but the gay Elia is not the Lamb who endured the madness of his sister, and her murder of their mother. It was only by adopting the mask of Elia that he could be gay and touching, paradoxical and sentimental.

His favourite writers were the dramatists and writers of the Jacobean period, and he had great knowledge and love of the theatre. His essay 'On some of the old actors' shows his understanding of the characters of the plays and the care with which he studied the actors' interpretation of them. By a cunning admixture of description, cross-cut with quotation, he produces a vivid evocation of the actual performance.

PAGE 102

De Quincey carried the cult of self-revelation to its highest degree of dramatisation. Like Coleridge he first took opium as an anodyne for a nervous ailment, but gradually increased the dose until he was taking some 8000 drops of laudanum a day. Though he managed to reduce his consumption of the drug, he was never wholly free from the need and desire for it. With his creative force diverted into dreams, he broke out of this dream world only by making it the subject of his art: not with the ironic detachment of Hazlitt, but with unchecked self-dramatisation. At times he purports to be warning the reader against the effects of the drug, but the total effect is of exultation in his splendid and terrible dreams. These are described in such detail that they are still of interest to pathologists.

He uses a highly poetic prose, falling at times into incantatory rhythms, at others reverting to simplicity. The *Confessions* first made his literary reputation, but his interests were many-sided; he studied German metaphysics and political economy, wrote a novel, and an account of the Lake poets as intimate and penetrating as that of Hazlitt.

PAGE 104

The most highly wrought prose of the period was that of Walter Savage Landor. Sent down from Oxford for his republican sympathies, eccentric and intractable, he lived almost entirely withdrawn from the world, for the most part in Italy, where he died. Though he was perhaps the most classical of these writers, his feeling for ancient cultures was tinged with romanticism, and he is less a classicist than a classical scholar.

His *Imaginary Conversations* range through all periods from the classical to his own time, and their tone varies from the satiric to the purely idyllic, evoking the climate of the periods and achieving dramatic tension within each episode. Often he adopted the *personae* to express his own views. In this episode his literary opinions emerge through the conversation between Southey, one of the Lake poets, and Porson, a Cambridge professor of Greek whose erudition and unceasing powers of conversation were the terror of his friends and undergraduates.

PAGE 107

Neither Lord Macaulay nor Thomas Carlyle can be called
objective historians. Carlyle was opposed to the lucidity of
French and English philosophers and took his stand with
the German transcendentalists. Rejecting political economy as a panacea for society, he advocated a reversal
to medievalism and the rule of strong men. Institutions
must be reformed by the regeneration of individuals,
inspired by the 'heroes' in whom was concentrated the
wisdom and spiritual power of mankind.

Poor, sensitive, and often boorish, Carlyle was married
to a woman of wit and intelligence, whose letters and
journals give an amusing picture of their often stormy
domestic life and their circle of friends. Carlyle's philosophy is no longer of very great interest, though the passion
with which it is expressed results in writing of great power
and occasional opacity. But his *French Revolution* has never
been surpassed as a re-creation of the period. With him
the sense of being not an onlooker but a participator in
the events is very strong. One is a revolutionary on the
Champ de Mars, a victim of Robespierre, a *tricoteuse* at the
execution of the king. The rather turgid prose of his
philosophic writing slides into simplicity; he achieves immediacy by the imaginative use of detail and by his power
of entering into the minds of his characters.

PAGE 109

Macaulay had the same capacity for entering into the
life of a period. His most sustained piece of writing is his
History of England, planned to extend from the reign of

James II to Queen Anne, but prevented by his death from reaching beyond the reign of William III. A barrister and a politician holding ministerial office, he was one of the main contributors to the *Edinburgh Review*. His essays and reviews combine his historical and literary methods.

When characters were sympathetic to him, he wrote of them with great discernment, but he is often partial, and when partial, unjust. As a Whig historian, the character of Charles II was anathema to him, and he writes of that intelligent and diplomatic monarch with total misunderstanding of his subtle policies. Nevertheless it is a fine piece of sustained condemnation. His style is carefully balanced, but the shortness of his periods sometimes gives an effect of jerkiness increased by his use of the full stop to punctuate his shorter phrases.

PAGE III

The story of the Brontë sisters is one of the strangest in the history of writing. Three of the five daughters of Patrick Brontë, the curate of Haworth, a remote village in the Yorkshire moors, were writers. Their poems under the pseudonyms of Currer, Ellis and Acton Bell were published first, and later their novels appeared under the same names. The two eldest daughters had died of consumption, and in 1848 Bramwell their dissolute brother died, to be followed a few months later by Emily, and in the following year by Anne, leaving Charlotte the sole survivor of six children.

There is no doubt that Emily was the most powerful novelist among them, as well as being a considerable poet.

She saw human beings lifted from the ruck of everyday life into an almost cosmic relationship with the universe; man and nature were part of the same natural forces, subject to the same urges, and free of human moral laws. The very name *Wuthering Heights* recalls the wild Yorkshire moors in all their moods, and the families she writes about are as wild and primitive as the moors: the waif Heathcliff brought to the farm by Mr Earnshaw; Catherine the young girl who loves him with an affinity beyond normal liking or passion, which she describes in this passage; her marriage to the gentle Edgar Linton; Heathcliff's revenge continuing beyond her death to destroy the second generation; the ghost of Catherine returning to haunt the only place where her spirit could find peace.

In its form the book is masterly: the opening description of the farm seen through the eyes of a stranger with the heightened awareness of the unfamiliar; the use of two narrators to run the past and present into one; the style with its lilting music and underlying tension. It is a book which it is hard to criticise and impossible to forget.

PAGE 114

Though Charlotte had not the cosmic imagination of Emily Brontë, she too had the power to quiet one's analytic mind, to make one forget the contrivances of her plots, the artificiality of some of her characters. She had an almost childlike sense of the terror which can lurk in everyday things, the demon in the drawing-room. *Villette*, the story of a young English governess in a Brussels school, creates the atmosphere of place as powerfully as *Wuthering*

Heights: the echoing classrooms, the dormitories sinister as a morgue without the chattering schoolgirls, the garden full of the scent of flowers and the sound of whispered assignations.

Her stories are perhaps a kind of wish-fulfilment. There is always the governess, withdrawn and lonely, dowdy amongst the gaieties of fashionable life, but gradually attracting the attention and finally the love of the hero. Mr Rochester, the demon-lover of *Jane Eyre,* is almost a character from a Gothic novel, but M. Emanuel, the testy warm-hearted schoolmaster in *Villette*, is one of the most convincing of her characters. Charlotte herself had taught in a school in Brussels and is thought to have been in love with the principal. In fiction, the story ends more happily; though the ending is ambiguous, it is probable that M. Emanuel returned to marry Lucy Snowe.

PAGE 117

When Dickens was asked how he conceived the idea of *Pickwick Papers,* he said 'I thought of Mr Pickwick'. And it is the individual people who matter in his books: teeming, jostling and talking in endless soliloquies; larger than life, each a quintessence—of hypocrisy, of fecklessness, of snobbery and self-deception—; eccentric, villainous, or surpassingly virtuous. That he rarely saw his characters with any subtlety or depth of understanding, that his plots are artificial and sometimes ludicrous, that his lapses into bathos are frequent is of no account; his creatures are supremely alive. About them lies the Dickens landscape, the London of fog, of the slow-moving river, the dark alleys and legal offices smelling of leather, the marshes and mud-flats of East Anglia, the Christmas-card landscape of Dingley Dell.

Dickens's childhood was spent in great penury, his father was imprisoned for debt, and Dickens himself worked for a time in a blacking factory. In his early twenties he became a journalist and political reporter, but *Pickwick Papers,* first published in twenty monthly numbers, was an immediate success. Thereafter Dickens knew neither failure nor financial worry, though his domestic life was disrupted by his romantic relationships. His books were regularly published in monthly numbers, and he gave public readings of his work in England and America, moving both himself and his auditors to tears in the more affecting passages.

He was moved to anger by any form of cruelty and social injustice, but it is false to think that social reform is the primary purpose of his books. He wanted to write about people, and he created his best puppets of the stuff from which he himself was made, the working people and the lower middle class submerged in genteel poverty and struggling to get out.

If he sometimes slithered into bathos, his tread was sure in comedy; his comic characters and comic scenes are free of irony, of satire or sentimentality. They are pure laughter. Sam Weller, Mr Pickwick's chirpy servant, is the Cockney in essence; pawky, at ease, he parries learned counsel's questions with wit and good humour, and adroitly manages not to admit whether he has seen his employer embracing his landlady. As a humorist, Dickens probably never did better than in his first book.

PAGE 120

Vanity Fair, A Novel without a Hero, is a novel satirising society and men and women in society, seen in the contrasting lives of the two 'heroines' who first meet as girls in Miss Pinkerton's Academy: Amelia, the petted daughter of a rich merchant family, gentle, weak, born to be deceived; and red-headed Becky, off-spring of an impoverished artist and a French dancer, clever, amusing and unscrupulous, the archetype of the female adventuress.

Like a graph the story plots the curve of their fortunes. Becky starts life as a governess, and failing to capture Jos Sedley, Amelia's brother, marries Rawdon Crawley, a cavalry officer; Amelia weds George Osborne, a young officer who ends an intrigue with Becky by his death at the battle of Waterloo. Amelia has a child and sinks into poverty; Becky by unscrupulous means which finally alienate her husband fights her way into high society in Paris and London. The book ends with Amelia marrying an old flame, and Becky after a period in the disreputable Bohemia where Jos Sedley finds her, achieves a respectable old age.

Thackeray made a precarious living as a journalist and caricaturist for many years in Paris and London, but the publication of *Vanity Fair,* his first novel, brought him into the first rank of novelists. He was the only one among them to obtrude his own personality as narrator, with apostrophes to the gentle reader, and ironic comments on the characters and episodes of his charade.

Though he saw more clearly than any other Victorian novelist the weakness and frailties of individuals, their vanities and self-deceptions, he sees them subject to the pressures of society. It is society that he condemns by implication and it is on Vanity Fair that he turns the full force of his irony. The picture of Becky, unscrupulously fighting her way into the *beau monde,* is in the main a sympathetic one; he sees her clearly but not unkindly. He does not esteem society highly enough not to be amused when it is deceived by wit, charm and gaiety, or trapped into giving its final *cachet* of respectability to an ageing courtesan in the guise of a charitable dowager.

PAGE 123

As the industrial revolution gradually changed the fabric of English society, writers began to declaim against the ugliness of the industrial world. The most passionate of them was Ruskin. He denounced the selfishness of an economic order which made the workman a slave to machinery and destroyed the nobility of labour. But his desire for social reform was only one aspect of his reaction against Victorian materialism. When he was a young man, angered by the ignorance revealed by critics of Turner's paintings, he wrote the first volume of his *Modern Painters.* Believing true art to be fidelity to an inner vision of reality such as he found in Turner's painting, he extolled the merits of his work in comparison with men like Claude and Poussin. Turner's paintings are described with precise evocation of the detail and complete understanding of the total effect. No painter has had such an apologist.

Over a period of seventeen years Ruskin wrote four more volumes of his *Modern Painters.* He dealt with many other painters, expounded his pantheistic philosophy, and included studies of natural landscape with its effects of light, rain and clouds. To read Ruskin is to see paintings with new perception and the countryside with fresh eyes. Sometimes his prose has the movement of a stormy sea; the phrases curve and break in waves, absorbing parentheses and clauses, and often achieving sentences of unwieldy length. But no writer on art has succeeded in communicating so intensely his own enthusiasm and love for painting.

PAGE 125

Towards the end of the century when Pater was evoking in chiselled prose the writers and painters of the Renaissance, the whole attitude of aesthetic criticism had changed. Ruskin had sought, through studying the organisation of appearances into works of art, to find a divine order and harmony in the universe. Pater was the prophet of the movement towards art for art's sake. Nothing is more typical of their differing attitudes than their lives in Oxford. Ruskin, Slade Professor of Art, organised undergraduates into road-making gangs to taste the pleasures of physical labour; Pater, Fellow of Brasenose, lived the life of a recluse, diffusing his message chiefly through his writings and his disciples.

His aesthetic faith was to direct every human soul towards 'burning with a hard gem-like flame'. The sole endeavour of human life was to submit with all the sensitivity and intensity at its command to every aesthetic and spiritual experience. A painting brought Pater into a state of ecstasy which detached itself from the original experience to float into mystic apprehensions. His style often transcends the barrier between prose and poetry, and breaks into the rhythms of verse. More disciplined than Ruskin's, more felicitous in its search for the exact word, it has a nervous power, but lacks Ruskin's pervading enthusiasm.

PAGE 127

The revolt against Victorian materialism took many forms. The Oxford Movement, started in Oxford by Keble, sought to rouse the Anglican church into a higher conception of its spiritual role. Amongst its leaders was John Henry Newman, a Fellow of Oriel and vicar of St Mary's, Oxford. In 1841 Newman published a tract to prove that the Thirty-nine Articles of the Church of England creed were compatible with Catholic doctrine. As he writes in this passage, the Movement was then banned; Newman resigned his living, and four years later joined the Church of Rome. As a priest, he established an Oratory in Birmingham, and when he was nearly eighty, was created a Cardinal.

The *Apologia* was written in response to an attack upon him by Charles Kingsley. In it he explains amongst other things, the reasons for his gradual rejection of the Church of England in favour of the Church of Rome. A man of great sensitivity, he was aware of the emotional as well as the logical implications of his decision. Without false pathos and self-pity, the mental struggle emerges through his limpid style. It is the spiritual history of a great and sincere man.

PAGE 130

'*Philistine* must have originally meant . . . a strong, dogged unenlightened opponent of the chosen people.' Thus Matthew Arnold defines the word which he was the first to use to express the insularity of English culture and its hostility to abstract ideas. In his literary criticism he initiated a new school which sought to form a set of coherent principles, based partly on classical precepts, partly on modern examples. He was the first critic to be influenced by French writers, and in judging writing he takes account of the finer shades of style and construction. Despite occasional lapses of sentiment and taste, his style has lucidity and an easy eloquence.

By profession an inspector of schools, he was a poet and professor of poetry at Oxford for ten years. In this preface to his critical essays he spares the 'beautiful city' from his general strictures against the philistinism of England.

PAGES 132, 134

George Eliot and Thomas Hardy are the outstanding rural novelists of the Victorian era. The two novels from which these passages are taken are studies of country girls at war with their environment, but there the similarity ends. Maggie, the heroine of *The Mill on the Floss,* headstrong, imaginative and intelligent, is stultified by the narrowness of provincial life. In an effort to find a soul-mate she wrecks the lives of several people, is herself compromised, and finally dies in an attempt to rescue her brother Tom, the one person whom she has consistently loved, from a flooding mill-race. Tess, a poor peasant, but of ancient lineage, is seduced by Alec d'Urberville, bears his child who dies, and later marries Angel Clare, the son of a clergyman. On their wedding-night she confesses her previous affair, is deserted by Angel, and goes to live with Alec. Clare's repentant return causes her to murder Alec, and after a period in hiding with Clare she is brought to justice and hanged.

Both Hardy and George Eliot were born and brought up in the country; George Eliot in Warwickshire, a lush county with large fields and slow-moving rivers, Hardy in Dorset with its gloomy tracts of moor, forests and rounded hills. Both understood the peasantry, though for George Eliot they were an ordered social hierarchy, and for Hardy primal beings closely bound to the earth. To George Eliot, a woman of great intellectual power, men and women were creatures moved by a desire for virtue and self-fulfilment, but often prevented by some flaw or weakness from attaining to it. She was the first English novelist to draw her characters in the grip of moral dilemmas, and to show the development of character under the stress of decision. At the same time she saw many of the country people with a gently satirical eye, as in this delicious episode of the melancholy Mrs Pullet and her new bonnet.

'Justice was done, and the President of the Immortals (in Aeschylean phrase) had ended his sport with Tess.' No free-will or moral decision could save Hardy's doomed characters; he saw them in the grip of their inevitable fate, subject to the blind injustices of the gods. The human flaw was there and irredeemable. Because of this he draws his characters with compassion and tenderness; not even the evil are wholly condemned. And the countryfolk, when they are not bowed by tragedy or need, are gay: dancing in country festivals, sitting in the harvest fields, or feasting in farm kitchens. Though he was writing when the industrial revolution had spawned mean towns over England, Hardy's country is primitive and unchanged, and he describes it with the delicate perceptions of a poet. After *Tess* he wrote only one novel of any length, and for the last thirty years of his life devoted himself to poetry.

PAGE 137

The English love nonsense. Lear's poems and limericks, the Alice books, Belloc's *Cautionary Tales,* are cherished in the nursery and quoted through life. The Alice books were written by Charles Dodgson, an Oxford mathematician, to beguile the long summer afternoons for Alice Liddell, the small daughter of the dean of his college. And Alice is the heroine; a small Victorian girl with flowing hair who moves with a child's remorseless logic through surrealist Looking-glass Land: a chessboard where 'it takes all the running you can do, to keep in the same place'. A chess problem is worked out in the course of the story, though the White Knight falls off his horse, the Red Queen is testy and dictatorial, and the White Queen, fat and vague, is always losing her hairpins.

PAGE 140

Few writers can tell a story better than Robert Louis Stevenson, and his story-telling is at its best when he sees through the eyes of a child. He sees the giant figures loom through the mist, the harsh voices, the inexplicable moods of grown-up people. *Treasure Island* is a perfect children's book. From the opening with its foreboding note of adventures to come, it moves fast and excitingly, crowded with incident and full of atmosphere. The story is told by the boy Jim Hawkins, son of the proprietor of the Admiral Benbow Inn, where an old buccaneer arrives with a map of a Pacific island where treasure is buried. The 'black spot' which means death is delivered to him by the blind Pew, as described in this passage. With his confederates Pew tries to find the map, but is outwitted by Jim who retrieves it. In company with the squire, the doctor, and the one-legged buccaneer Long John Silver, he sets out for the island and, after a number of adventures, finds the treasure.

Stevenson had a sense of vocation which caused him to train himself by imitating other writers, 'playing the sedulous ape' as he called it; his care for the art of writing is more French than English. Born in Edinburgh, he was driven by ill health to live in the South Seas, where he died at the age of forty-four with his greatest book *Weir of Hermiston* unfinished. The Samoans amongst whom he lived called him 'Tusitala' or the teller of tales.

PAGE 143

In his long life Meredith linked the two chief movements of the nineteenth century. His first wife was the daughter of Thomas Love Peacock, the witty and ironic friend of Shelley; the Pre-Raphaelites were his friends, and he lodged for a time with both Swinburne and Rossetti. But his writing partakes of the manner of the French impressionists, and the outlines of his characters emerge from an intensity of flickering light. With an intelligence which probes the subtler nuances of behaviour, and with irony softened by romantic imagination, he studies the problem of a character overweighted by a pathological *humour*, egoism. The egoist, Sir Willoughby Patterne, handsome, rich, jilted by one young woman, wins Miss Middleton, to lose her again by his demanding conceit. The book is the story of her struggle to free herself.

Meredith's women are throw-backs to the heroines of Restoration comedies: witty, intelligent and gay, breaking out of the cocoon of Victorian male domination. Clara Middleton, here described, eventually marries Vernon Whitford, 'Phoebus Apollo turned fasting friar', a character based on Leslie Stephen, the father of Virginia Woolf. The interplay of characters is revealed in a series of intuitive revelations as brilliant as the epigrammatic summings-up of Mrs Mountstuart Jenkinson; but the flashes often serve to emphasise the pervading obscurity. Meredith's readers need intelligence and determination.

PAGE 145

It is fitting that the last book should be aimed at the whole pious façade of the Victorian family. Butler was the son and the grandson of clergymen, and his novel is largely autobiographical. The story ranges through several generations of the Pontifex family. From John Pontifex the village carpenter to his grandson Theobald who is jockeyed into becoming a clergyman and marrying Christina. Their son Ernest after a miserable childhood of parental tyranny, breaks out into a disastrous marriage and is only saved by a fortune inherited from an aunt, which enables him to become a writer.

With irony and wit attaining almost to the urbane savagery of Swift, Butler describes life in a Victorian family: the values basically material, the pharisaical hypocrisy, the self-deceptions. His dissection of motives is pitiless, his intention patricide.

GLOSSARY

A—, *sb.* arse, rump, 70
Abused, *v.t.* misused, 15, 38
Aerolite, *sb.* meteorite, 106
Ambs ace, *sb.* double ace, the lowest throw in dice , 19

Bavarian poke, *sb.* goitre, 29
Bewray, *v.t.* reveal, divulge, 16
Bloody-fallen, *adj.* chilblained, 29
Bob, *sb.* larva of the beetle, 32
Bombast, *sb.* inflated language, 53
Brickbat, *sb.* part of a brick, often used as a missile, 59
Bug-bear, *sb.* bogy, groundless fear, 35

Camelion, *sb.* chameleon, 98
Cap, *sb.* a drinking vessel, 51
Carcanet, *sb.* necklace, 30
Carrack, *sb.* ship, galleon, 30
Case, *sb.* condition, plight, 4
Case-worm, *sb.* caddis-worm, larva of the May-fly, 32
Cast, *v.t.* resolve, contrive, 2
Caul, *sb.* membrane sometimes covering a child's head at birth, believed to be a preventative against drowning, 143
Chapless, *adj.* without the lower jaw, or without the fleshy part of the jaw, 25
Charnel-house, *sb.* vault or repository for the bones of the dead, 24, 105
Cheer, *sb.* face, expression of the face, 5
Cheven, *sb.* another name for the chub, 31
Chimera, *sb.* a fanciful idea, an idea without foundation, 37
Chitty-face, *sb.* a thin pinched face, 28
Cithern, *sb.* a kind of guitar, similar to the zithern, 12
Clench, *sb.* pun, 53
Cod-worm, *sb.* caddis-worm, larva of the May-fly, 32
Coil, *sb.* fuss, ado, 19
Conceit, *v.t.* imagine, 19
Course, by, *adv.* by custom, customarily, 7, 9
Covenant, *sb.* the Covenant entered into by the Scottish Presbyterians with the English Government in 1643, 110

Cowturd, *sb.* piece of cow-dung, 32

Cun, *v.t.* con, to direct the steering of a ship, 74

Curious, *adj.* careful, solicitous, 17

Danegelt, *sb.* land-tax originally imposed to raise funds to protect England against the Danes, 39

Descension, *sb.* the setting of the sun below the horizon, 36

Despite, *sb.* scorn, disdain, 16

Discommon, *v.t.* in Oxford and Cambridge, to take away from a tradesman the right of trading with undergraduates, 128

Disport, *sb.* amusement, diversion, 16

Diuturnity, *sb.* long duration, lastingness, 36

Dolour, *sb.* lamentation, 3

Domino, *sb.* a loose cloak, usually worn to a masked ball, 121

Dor, *sb.* black-beetle, 32

Dug, *sb.* breast, 29

Dunstable, *adj.* plain, direct; from the town of Dunstable on the Roman road from London to the north, 20

Encomiast, *sb.* one who praises something very highly, 57

Eschew, *v.t.* avoid, 4

Exolution, *sb.* setting-free, relaxation, 37

Extasis, *sb.* mystical trance, 37

Fare, *sb.* fuss, commotion, 1

Fight, *sb.* screen to protect fighting men on board ship, 9

Flesh-fly, *sb.* blow-fly which lays its eggs in dead flesh, 32

Flexure, *sb.* flexibility, 33

Flimflam, *sb.* nonsense, humbug, 70

Flip, *sb.* a drink, a mixture of beer and spirits, sweetened with sugar and heated, 95

Fricassée, *sb.* a dish of meat sliced and cooked in a sauce, 60

Fustilugs, *sb.* a fat, frowzy woman, 29

Gin, *(v.t.)* given, 71

Gubber-tushed, *adj.* having irregular, projecting teeth, 28

Gustation, *sb.* the act of tasting, 37

Handsel, *sb.* the first money taken by a trader, or the first instalment of a payment, 57

Haul upon a wind, *v.t.* to bring a ship round to sail closer to the wind, 74

Hempdressers, *sb.* the name of a country dance, 82

Hoddypeak, *adj.* foolish, 20

Howboy, *sb.* hautbois, an instrument similar to the present-day oboe, 12

Incondite, *adj.* unrefined, 29

Incontinent, *adv.* immediately, at once, 4

Incurvetting, *adj.* curving inwards, 50

Iniquity, *sb.* adverse fate or injustice, 35

Lave-eared, *adj.* having drooping ears, 29

Lay along, *v.i.* to come alongside, 74

Lee-brace, *sb.* the rope attached to a sail on the lee side of a ship; *see also under* set, 74

Let, *sb.* hindrance, 8

Licorous, *adj.* wanton, desirous, 18

Liquefaction, *sb.* reduction to a liquid state, the 'melting' of the soul, 37

Lochaber-axe, *sb.* a large axe with a hook behind the blade, 92

Lucina, *sb.* goddess of childbirth, hence midwife, 36

Lust, *sb.* appetite, desire, 3

Make up a market, *v.i.* to make a profit, 20

Mandrake, *sb.* a root, supposed to shriek when removed from the ground, 25

Mard, *sb.* piece of excrement, 29

Margent, *sb.* margin, 14

Mean, in the mean season, *adv.* in the meantime, 3

Mew, *v.t.* when referring to a bird of prey, to moult; probably used here poetically as a symbol of renewal of youth, 38

Minish, *v.t.* remove, 5

moles, *sb.* Roman mausoleum or monument, 37

Mome, *sb.* a fool, 15

Momus, *sb.* the god of ridicule; hence a harsh critic, a fault-finder, 15

Nut, *adv.* not, 70

Oaf, *sb.* a deformed person, 29

Odd's, *sb.* used in oaths instead of 'God's', 73

Ollio, *sb.* a dish of various meats cooked together, hence a hotch-potch, 60

Overset, *v.t.* overturn, capsize, 74

Partisan, *sb.* long-handled spear, 92

Pass, *v.t.* to surpass or excel, 2, 7, 12

Playing in flush, *v.i.* in card games, playing a whole hand of cards of the same suit, 82

Plum, *adj.* delicious, or, possibly, plump, 18

Post, *adv.* rapidly, hastily, 13

Predicament, *sb.* assertion of ideas, in logic or philosophy, 37

Puppie, *sb.* a doll, a doll-like woman (from 'puppet'), 19

Quaff, *v.t.* to drink deeply, 95

Quean, *sb.* wanton, loose woman, 29

Quit, quitted, *v.t.* reprieve, freed, 35

Ragoust, *sb.* ragoût; dish of meat cut into small pieces, 60

Raise a perpendicular, *v.t.* to draw a line at right angles to another line, here probably refferring to plotting the cours of a ship, 75

Rammy, *adj.* having a bad, rank smell, 29

Ravin, *sb.* the seizing of food or prey, 7

Rawbone, *sb.* gaunt or lean person, 29

Repiningly, *adv.* discontentedly, 18

Run your rig, *v.t.* to run riot, to play pranks, 75

Scabbed, *adj.* covered with scabs or sores, 29

Scape, *v.t.* escape, 4

Seethe, *v.t.* to boil, 7

Set in the lee-brace, *v.t.* to fix in position the rope attached to the sail on the lee side of a ship, 74

She, *sb.* woman, 20

Sith, sithen, *conj.* since, 2, 14

Soul-heal, *sb.* salvation, 1

Spittle, *sb.* hospital, 26

Splay-footed, *adj.* having feet which turn outwards, 29

Splice a rope, *v.t.* to join ropes by untwisting and reweaving the strands, 75

Squis'd, *adj.* squeezed, squashed, 28

Surety, *sb.* safety, security, 4

Tabby, *sb.* silk taffeta, originally striped, hence tabby-cat, 49
Tit, *sb.* a young woman, a huzzy, 29
Towardly, *adj.* good, tractable, 32
Truss, *sb.* a bundle of hay, 39

Vile, *adj.* base, humble, 7
Viol, *sb.* an instrument similar to the violin, but having five or six
    strings, 12
Virago, *sb.* a scolding woman, 29

Wit you, *v.t.* you must know, 2
Wrack, *sb.* disaster, ruin, 2
Wunt = would not, 70

Zoodikers, an oath, probably 'God's workers', cf. odd's, 70

A LIST OF THE MOST ACCESSIBLE
EDITIONS

(Prices refer to 1 June 1956 and are liable to alteration)

ADDISON, Joseph, Richard Steele and others. *The Spectator*. Dent (Everyman's Library, 164–7). 4 vols. 5s. each. (Text from the edition of Thomas Tickell.)

ARNOLD, Matthew. *Essays in Criticism*. Macmillan. Out of print.

AUBREY, John. *Brief Lives*, ed. by O. Lawson Dick. 1949. Secker and Warburg. Reprinting.

AUSTEN, Jane, *Emma*. Oxford University Press (World's Classics, 129). 5s.

BACON, Francis, Lord Verulam. *Essays, Civil and Moral*. Oxford University Press (World's Classics, 24). 5s.

BERNERS, John Bourchier, Lord. *Sir John Froissart: Chronicles of England, France, Spain*. ed. by W. P. Ker. 1927–8. Blackwell (Shakespeare Head Press). 8 vols. Out of print.

BOSWELL, James. *Life of Samuel Johnson*. Oxford University Press (Standard Authors). 2 vols. in 1. 21s.

BRONTË, Charlotte. *Villette*. Dent (Everyman's Library, 351). 5s.

BRONTË, Emily. *Wuthering Heights*. Dent (Everyman's Library, 243). 6s.

BROWNE, Sir Thomas. *Urn Burial*, included in *Religio Medici etc*. Dent (Everyman's Library, 92). 5s.

BUNYAN, John. *The Pilgrim's Progress*. Oxford University Press (World's Classics, 12). 5s.

BURKE, Edmund. *Reflections on the French Revolution*. Dent (Everyman's Library, 460). 6s.

BURTON, Robert. *The Anatomy of Melancholy*. Dent (Everyman's Library, 886–8). 3 vols. 5s each.

BUTLER, Samuel. *The Way of all Flesh*. Dent (Everyman's Library, 895). 6s.

CARLYLE, Thomas. *The French Revolution*. Dent (Everyman's Library, 31, 32). 2 vols. 6s. each. (Text from 1st ed.)

CARROLL, Lewis. *Through the Looking-glass*. Macmillan. 6s.

CLARENDON, Edward Hyde, Earl of. *History of the Great Rebellion*, edited by W. D. Macray. 1888. Oxford University Press. 6 vols. Binding; or *Selections*, edited by G. Huehns. Oxford University Press (World's Classics, 544). 8s. 6d,

COLERIDGE, Samuel Taylor: *Biographia Literaria*. Dent (Everyman's Library, 11). 7s.

DEFOE, Daniel: *Colonel Jack*. 1947. H. Hamilton (Novel Library). 6*s*.

DEKKER, Thomas. *The Wonderfull Yeare 1603*, ed. by G. B. Harrison. 1924. Lane; out of print. Or in *Three Elizabethan Pamphlets*, ed. by G. R. Hibbard. 1951. Harrap. 7*s*. 6*d*.

DICKENS, Charles. *Pickwick Papers*. Oxford University Press (Oxford Illustrated Dickens). 10*s*. 6*d*.

DONNE, John. *Complete Poems and Selected Prose,* ed. by John Hayward. 1950. Faber (Nonesuch Library). 21*s*.

DRYDEN, John. *An Essay of Dramatick Poesy* (and other essays). Dent (Everyman's Library, 568). 6*s*.

ECCLESIASTES, Book of, in the Authorised Version of the Bible. Many editions of the Authorised Version are published by the Oxford University Press and Cambridge University Press from 6*s*. upwards.

ELIOT, George. *The Mill on the Floss*. Dent (Everyman's Library, 325). 5*s*.

FIELDING, Henry. *Tom Jones*. Dent (Everyman's Library, 355, 356). 2 vols. 6*s*. each.

GIBBON, Edward. *The Decline and Fall of the Roman Empire,* ed. by O. Smeaton. Dent (Everyman's Library, 434–6, 474–6). 6 vols. 7*s*. each.

HAKLUYT, Richard. *Principal Navigations*. Dent (Illustrated Classics). 10 vols. Out of print. (Text from *Voyages of the Elizabeth Seamen*, ed. by C. R. Beazley. 1893. Oxford University Press.)

HARDY, Thomas. *Tess of the d'Urbervilles*. Macmillan (Pocket edition). 6*s*.

HAZLITT, William. *Selected Essays,* ed. by Geoffrey Keynes. 1949. Faber (Nonesuch Library). 21*s*.

JOHNSON, Samuel. *Lives of the English Poets*. Dent (Everyman's Library, 770, 771). 2 vols. 6*s*. each.

KEATS, John. *Letters,* ed. by M. Buxton Forman. 4th ed. 1952. Oxford University Press. 35*s*.; or *Letters*, selected by Frederick Page. 1954. Oxford University Press (World's Classics, 541). 8*s*. 6*d*.

LAMB, Charles. *Essays of Elia*. Dent (Everyman's Library, 14). 6*s*.

LANDOR, Walter Savage. *Imaginary Conversations and Poems,* ed. by Charles C. Crump. 1891. Dent, 6 vols. Out of print.

LYLY, John. *Euphues and his England* in the Complete Works of John Lyly, ed. by R. W. Bond. 1902. Oxford University Press. 3 vols. 105*s*.

MACAULAY, Thomas Babington, Lord Macaulay. *Critical and Historical Essays*. Dent (Everyman's Library, 225, 226). 2 vols. 5*s*. each.

MALORY, Sir Thomas. *Le Morte d'Arthur*. Dent (Everyman's Library, 45, 46). 2 vols. 6s. each.

MEREDITH, George. *The Egoist*. Oxford University Press (World's Classics, 508). 8s. 6d.

MILTON, John. *Areopagitica* (and other prose). Dent (Everyman's Library, 795). 6s.

MORE, Sir Thomas. *Utopia*, trans. by R. Robynson. 1904. Oxford University Press. 7s. 6d.

NASHE, Thomas. *The Unfortunate Traveller*, included in *Shorter Novels*, vol. 1 (Elizabethan). Dent (Everyman's Library, 824). 6s.

NEWMAN, John Henry. *Apologia pro vita sua*. Dent (Everyman's Library, 636). 6s.

NORTH, Sir Thomas: *Plutarch's Lives of the Noble Grecians and Romans*, translated from the French of J. Amyot. 1929-30. Nonesuch Press. 5 vols. Out of print.

PATER, Walter. *The Renaissance*. Macmillan. Out of print.

PEPYS, Samuel. *Diary*, ed. by H. B. Wheatley. Reprinted 1949. G. Bell. 8 vols. in 3. 84s. (Text from 1825 Braybrooke edition, Everyman's Library. Out of print.)

QUINCEY, Thomas de. *Confessions of an English Opium Eater*. Dent (Everyman's Library, 223). 5s.

RICHARDSON, Samuel. *Clarissa*. Dent (Everyman's Library, 882-5). 4 vols. 5s. each.

RUSKIN, John. *Modern Painters*. Dent (Everyman's Library, 208-212). 5 vols. 208-9, 5s each; 210-12 out of print.

SCOTT, Sir Walter. *The Heart of Mid-Lothian*. Dent (Everyman's Library, 134). 7s.

SIDNEY, Sir Philip. *An Apologie for Poetrie*, included in *The Prelude to Poetry*, ed. by Ernest Rhys. Dent (Everyman's Library, 789). 5s.

SMOLLETT, Tobias. *Peregrine Pickle*. Dent (Everyman's Library, 838, 839). 2 vols. 7s. each.

STERNE, Laurence. *Tristram Shandy*. Dent (Everyman's Library, 617). 7s.

STEVENSON, Robert Louis. *Treasure Island*. Oxford University Press (World's Classics, 295). 5s.

SWIFT, Jonathan. *Selected Writings in Prose and Verse*. Faber (Nonesuch Library). 21s.

TAYLOR, Jeremy. *Holy Dying*. Reprinted by Longmans; out of print. Dent (Temple Classics); out of print.

THACKERAY, William Makepeace. *Vanity Fair*. Dent (Everyman's Library, 298). 5s.

TRAHERNE, Thomas. *Centuries of Meditations.* Reprinted 1950. Dobell; out of print.

WALPOLE, Horace, Earl of Orford. *Letters,* ed. by Mrs Paget Toynbee. 1903–5. Supplement 1918–25. Oxford University Press, 16+3 vols. Out of print.

WALTON, Izaak. *The Compleat Angler.* Oxford University Press (World's Classics, 430). 6s.